CHARCUTERIE

PÂTÉS, TERRINES, SAVORY PIES

Project Coordinator, FERRANDI Paris: Audrey Janet
Chefs, FERRANDI Paris: Marc Alès (Meilleur Ouvrier de France 2000), Stéphane Jakic, and Frédéric Lesourd
Students, FERRANDI Paris: Igor Tauber and Dionysis Dimitroulis

French Edition
Design and Typesetting: Alice Leroy
Editorial Collaboration: Estérelle Payany
Editorial Director: Ronite Tubiana
Editor: Clélia Ozier-Lafontaine, assisted by Marie Poulain

English Edition
Editorial Director: Kate Mascaro
Editor: Helen Adedotun
Translation from the French: Ansley Evans
Copyediting: Wendy Sweetser
Typesetting: Alice Leroy
Proofreading: Nicole Foster
Indexing: JMS/Chris Bell
Cover Design: Audrey Sednaoui

Production: Julie Hautecourt
Color Separation: IGS-CP, L'Isle d'Espagnac
Printed in China by Toppan Leefung

Simultaneously published in French as *Terrines, Pâtés en Croûte, Rillettes, Charcuteries...: Recettes et Techniques d'une École d'Excellence*

Éditions Flammarion, S.A.
82 Rue Saint-Lazare
CS 10124
75009 Paris
France
editions.flammarion.com

22 23 24 3 2 1
ISBN: 978-2-08-029467-8
Legal Deposit: 10/2022

FERRANDI

PARIS

RECIPES AND TECHNIQUES FROM THE FERRANDI SCHOOL OF CULINARY ARTS

Photography by Rina Nurra

Flammarion

PREFACE

For over one hundred years, **FERRANDI Paris** has taught all of the culinary disciplines to students from around the world. Following the success of our four previous works published by Flammarion—a comprehensive guide to the art of French pâtisserie, as well as volumes focused on cooking with chocolate, vegetables, and fruit and nuts—it is now time to explore the French art of charcuterie. This centuries-old craft offers a whole host of techniques and creative recipe ideas. Pâtés, terrines, savory pies, and stuffings—whether made with meat, fish, or vegetables—are enjoying a renaissance and have resumed their rightful place in haute cuisine. This art is part of the French culinary heritage that **FERRANDI Paris** teachers are committed to keeping alive.

Both traditional skills and creative innovation lie at the heart of **FERRANDI Paris**'s teaching philosophy. We maintain a balance between the two through strong ties to the professional world, making our school a leading institution in the field.

That is why this book not only provides delicious recipes, but also demonstrates fundamental techniques and shares expert advice. Anyone who wishes to explore the inspiring world of charcuterie, whether it be at home or in a professional kitchen, will find this volume an invaluable reference.

I extend my warmest thanks to those members of **FERRANDI Paris** who have brought this book to fruition, particularly Audrey Janet, who coordinated the project, and Marc Alès (Meilleur Ouvrier de France 2000), Stéphane Jakic, and Frédéric Lesourd, chefs at the school who have generously shared their expertise and adeptly combined technical skills and creativity to demonstrate the rich culinary potential of French charcuterie.

Richard Ginioux
Executive Director of FERRANDI Paris

CONTENTS

INTRODUCTION

A Portrait of **FERRANDI Paris**

In over one hundred years of history, **FERRANDI Paris** has earned an international reputation as one of the premier culinary and hospitality schools in France. Since its inception, the school—hailed "the Harvard of gastronomy" by the press—has trained generations of groundbreaking chefs and entrepreneurs who have left their mark in the industry around the world. Whether at its historic campus in the Saint-Germain-des-Prés neighborhood in Paris, or its campus in Saint-Gratien, Bordeaux, Rennes, or Dijon, this institution is dedicated to world-class teaching with the aim of training future leaders in the culinary and pastry arts, hotel and restaurant management, and hospitality entrepreneurship.

Founded more than a century ago by the Paris Île-de-France Regional Chamber of Commerce and Industry, **FERRANDI Paris** is the only school in France to offer the full range of degree and certification programs in the culinary and hospitality arts, from vocational training to the master's degree level, in addition to international programs. The school takes pride in its 98 percent exam pass rate, which is the highest in France for degrees and certifications in the sector. No matter the level, a **FERRANDI Paris** education is rigorous and combines mastering the basics with an emphasis on innovation, management and entrepreneurial skills, and hands-on practice in a professional environment.

Strong Ties to the Professional World

A space for discovery, inspiration, and exchange—where the culinary arts mingle with science, technology, and innovation—**FERRANDI Paris** brings together the biggest names in the sector to discuss and shape the future of the hospitality industry and push the boundaries of culinary creativity. The school trains 2,200 apprentices and students each year, in addition to three hundred international students of over thirty nationalities and two thousand adults who come to the school to perfect their skills or change careers. The hundred instructors at the school are all highly qualified: several have received prominent culinary awards and distinctions, such as the Meilleur Ouvrier de France title (Best Craftsman in France), and all have at least ten years of work experience in the culinary field in prestigious establishments in France and abroad. To give students maximum opportunities and the chance to connect with other fields and the greater global community, the school has formed collaborative partnerships with several other institutions. In France, partner schools include the ESCP Europe Business School, AgroParisTech, and the Institut Français de la Mode; abroad, the school collaborates with Johnson and Wales University in the United States, the ITHQ tourism and hotel management school in Canada, the Hong Kong Polytechnic University, and the Institute for Tourism Studies in China, among others. Since theory and practice go hand in hand, and because **FERRANDI Paris** strives for excellence in teaching,

students also have the chance to participate in a number of official events through partnerships with several chief culinary associations in France, including Maîtres Cuisiniers de France, Société des Meilleurs Ouvriers de France, Euro-Toques, and more. In addition, the school offers numerous prestigious professional competitions and prizes, giving students many opportunities to demonstrate their skills and knowledge. A dedicated ambassador of French culture, **FERRANDI Paris** draws students from around the world every year and is a member of the French Interministerial Tourism Council; the Strategic Committee of Atout France (the French tourism development agency); and the Conférence des Formations d'Excellence au Tourisme (CFET), a group of institutions in France offering top-quality training in tourism-related fields.

Extensive Savoir Faire

FERRANDI Paris's expertise, combining practice and close collaboration with professionals in the field, has been shared in four previous volumes—one devoted to French pâtisserie, one to chocolate making, the third to vegetables, and the fourth to fruits and nuts—intended for both professional chefs and amateur cooks. Following the success of these four books—Pâtisserie received a Gourmand World Cookbook award—**FERRANDI Paris** has now turned its attention to the art of charcuterie. This newest addition to the collection offers traditional and modern takes on specialties including pâtés, pâtés en croûte, terrines, rillettes, savory pies, stuffings, and more.

Terrines, Pâtés, Pies, Sausages, and Other Charcuterie Dishes

While charcutiers have historically specialized in "cooked meats" (the literal meaning of "charcuterie"), their craft has expanded to include fish and vegetables—all prepared with little to no waste, using time-honored techniques. For the charcutier, every part of the animal is valuable, from the nose to the tail. Sausage meat is used to stuff paupiettes or vegetables, sausages are tucked into brioche, and well-honed seasonings make all the difference. Today, traditional country and liver pâtés are right at home alongside seasonal vegetable terrines, and the classic pork rillettes can be adapted into fish, duck, and even plant-based versions. In this book, **FERRANDI Paris** chefs share their inspiration and invite you to explore the incredible possibilities of charcuterie in recipes that are guaranteed to surprise and delight in equal measure. It's now your turn to head to the kitchen and discover the timelessness of this age-old craft.

CHARCUTERIE: THE ESSENTIALS

Pâtés, terrines, sausages, rillettes, and *farcis* (stuffed dishes) are all part of the big charcuterie family. In this book, **FERRANDI Paris** professionals share their secrets for successfully making both classic and updated versions of these iconic French preparations. The charcutier's craft is as old as that of the chef and involves its own particular set of techniques, yet the trade has also evolved to keep up with the times, embracing new ingredients and even plant-based variations. This introduction offers an overview of French charcuterie, including basic definitions to ensure success in the recipes that follow.

The origins of charcuterie

The profession of charcutier was officially born in France in 1475, when the Prévôté de Paris, representing the French crown, authorized the first master *chayrcuitiers, saucissiers, boudiniers* (sic) to ply their trade. Raw meat was the butcher's domain, while cooked meat (the literal meaning of charcuterie) and pork butchery fell to the charcutier. Yet far earlier traces of the profession have been found. The *porcella* law, for instance, regulated the transformation of pork products—from rearing to selling—under the Roman Empire. Originally, the charcutier's job was to master salting and smoking to make meats suitable for long-term preservation. The profession has evolved over time, incorporating skills from butchers, chefs, and even pastry chefs. The art and craft of charcuterie thus combines the techniques of several culinary professions.

1. According to the *Dictionnaire de la Viande* (Dictionary of Meat) by the Académie de la Viande (the Meat Academy) (Éditions Autres Voix, 2012).

Classic and modern charcuterie

Charcuterie is defined as "varied meat preparations, often made with pork and offal, but also poultry, veal, beef, and sometimes fish and shellfish. The goal of charcuterie has long been to produce a variety of products and dishes that can be stored for a long time."[1] French charcuterie encompasses a remarkable variety of textures, shapes, and recipes—from smooth-textured pâtés, terrines, mousses, and rillettes, to roughly chopped, cooked, cured, or sliceable preparations (sausages, cured hams, etc.). All kinds of products fall under the charcuterie umbrella: cooked charcuterie; offal-based charcuterie; cured cooked meats; cured uncooked meats; dried cured meats; and so on. Beyond meat, fish and vegetables are now legitimate ingredients in the charcutier's craft, and spices or recipes from further afield continue to inspire innovative takes on traditional specialties.

Different types of charcuterie

France has over four hundred charcuterie specialties—nearly as many as there are cheeses or wines. Some are even centuries old. While this book does not include certain preparations intended for professionals (such as andouillettes and cured meats), it contains many others that are suitable for preparation in home kitchens. Here are the main categories you will find in this book.

Pies, tarts, and pâtés en croûte

Pâté literally means "cooked in a pastry crust (*pâte*)." The original pâtés were always "en croûte," akin to the English pie, and were served either hot or cold. Over time, the word evolved to designate the contents of the pie, without the crust. This chapter includes preparations that reflect the original meaning of the term: pâté en croûte, savory pies and tarts, pithiviers, coulibiac, and sausage in brioche. These are sometimes categorized as "*charcuteries pâtissières*" (i.e., charcuterie-filled pastries).

Pâtés and terrines

The word "terrine" denotes a preparation that has been cooked and chilled in a recipient of the same name, typically ceramic or porcelain—two materials that conduct heat well. Terrines come in countless varieties: they may be made with meat (pork, veal, poultry, or game), fish, or vegetables, and the texture can vary. Today, the terms terrine and pâté are often used interchangeably for preparations that were once baked in a pastry crust but are now cooked in a terrine mold. Pâtés *en terrine* may be smooth (such as liver pâté) or rustic (like country pâté), with larger pieces of meat. Terrines can also be pressed and weighted to make them more compact, known as pressés in French. The most famous pressés include Burgundy's *jambon persillé* (ham and parsley terrine) and *fromage de tête* (brawn or head cheese). Placing a weight on top releases the juices, which set when chilled, resulting in a firm texture suitable for slicing.

Rillettes and pulled meats and fish

Rillettes are traditionally made with meat—usually pork, veal, or poultry—cooked slowly in duck or goose fat or lard over many hours, until fall-apart tender. The meat is then shredded, mixed with the cooking fat, and stored in a mold. Rillettes have been appreciated in France for their tender, melt-in-the-mouth texture since at least the mid-eighteenth century. This preservation technique has evolved to incorporate fish and/or vegetables, using less fat and transforming the ingredients into delicious spreads, often called *éffilochés* in French.

Stuffed dishes

The broad category of charcuterie also encompasses many stuffed dishes, known as *farcis* in French—from the verb *farcir* (to stuff). The charcutier's typical stuffing—farce (see glossary p. 21)—is made with ground meat, fish, or vegetables blended with seasonings and sometimes a binding agent (usually bread, egg, or a starch) and other flavorings. Highly versatile, farce is one of the foundations of charcuterie. In the "Stuffed Dishes" chapter, it is used to stuff poultry; pieces of meat (in the case of paupiettes and ballotines, for instance); seafood (such as stuffed squid); vegetables (like zucchini); or even less popular cuts (including duck necks).

Cooked charcuterie

Finally, charcuterie plays a starring role in many other recipes in this book, which also take advantage of all the cuts of pork, veal, or beef—including cheeks, ears, tongues, or feet, depending on the animal. These charcuterie-based recipes not only reduce waste, but are also delicious.

Selecting meats

Among the 350 breeds of pig classified worldwide, about ten are produced in France, and most of this production (70 percent) goes to the French charcuterie industry. Classic breeds such as Large White, Landrace, and Duroc are particularly prized for their yield. On a smaller scale, artisan charcutiers continue to make unique regional charcuterie specialties with local heritage breeds, including West French White, Bayeux, Noir de Bigorre (also known as Gascon), Cul Noir Limousin, Kintoa (Basque black-pied pigs), and Nustrale from Corsica. The way in which animals are raised significantly influences the quality of their meat. Pasture-raised pigs have healthier, more flavorful fat, which impacts the overall taste of the meat, so purchase pastured pork products whenever you can. The same goes for beef: always buy grass-fed, if possible. For rabbits, poultry, and game, try to find artisan producers. In all cases—whether using meat, fish, or vegetables—be sure to use products at their prime. Many of the recipes in this book will keep for longer and will be better preserved if made with the freshest possible ingredients.

Salt, sugar, and herbs

The recipes in this book do not contain artificial additives or preservatives. They call for salt, spices, herbs, and sometimes even sugar, for preservation purposes and flavor.

What is salt used for and which should I choose?

Salt plays three roles in charcuterie:

- As a flavor enhancer, it is crucial to the final taste.
- It limits the development of certain germs and bacteria.
- It helps proteins bind together and thus indirectly contributes to texture.

Different types of salt used in this book:

- Unrefined coarse grey sea salt (7 percent impurities), rich in minerals, is best for salting water and broths for cooking and for preparing brine.
- Refined fine sea salt (less than 1 percent impurities), with a small grain that dissolves completely, makes it possible to season preparations perfectly with more homogeneous results.
- Fleur de sel should be used as a finishing salt to add a burst of texture and flavor.
- If using kosher salt, keep in mind that different brands have different flake sizes, so weighing it is more accurate than measuring it by volume.

If a particular type of salt is not specified, use fine salt, preferably sea salt.

Herbs and spices

Herbs and spices are essential ingredients in the charcutier's kitchen. Fresh parsley is the most commonly used herb in this book. Bay leaves and thyme are essential for broths, and rosemary is often used with rabbit. You won't need too many spices on hand to make the recipes in this book, but make sure they are fresh to ensure the best possible flavor. Juniper berries and coriander seeds season certain terrines, while spices like nutmeg and the French quatre-épices spice mix (ground pepper, cloves, nutmeg, and ginger) add depth to farces. Other spices to have on hand include whole cloves, *piment d'Espelette*, paprika, curry, and different types of black and white pepper for variety.

What is sugar used for?

In some foie gras and pâté recipes, the addition of small amounts of sugar (about ⅕ oz. per lb./4–5 g per kg) may come as a surprise. In the case of foie gras, this can compensate for the liver's natural bitterness, but is not essential if the recipe contains a sweet wine, which contains more sugar than dry alcohols. Sugar also serves to balance out different flavors, acting as a flavor enhancer and extending the finish on the tongue. In recipes containing ascorbic acid for color or preservation purposes, sugar helps to conceal the sour taste.

And alcohols?

Wines and other spirits are often used to marinate meats or boost flavor. Red or white wine, cognac, armagnac, Calvados, Madeira, and port wine are the most often used. They not only enhance taste, but also add a little sugar, which is always important to keep in mind when seasoning.

Glossary of Charcuterie Terms

Some of the charcuterie ingredients in this book may be unfamiliar to you. Here are some definitions to help you talk like the pros!

***BARDE*:** Very thinly sliced pork fatback, which charcutiers use to line terrine molds, wrap around roasts (called barding), and/or prevent certain preparations from drying out during cooking.

CASINGS, NATURAL (*menu*): Edible natural cases used for preparations such as sausages, made from the small intestine of various animals (cows, hogs, sheep, etc.). Casings are often sold according to their diameter, expressed in millimeters. For instance, a 34/36 casing has a diameter of 1⅓–1½ in. (34–36 mm). Plant-based and synthetic alternatives are available for meatless preparations.

CAUL FAT (*crépine*): A neutral-tasting pork or beef membrane used to wrap preparations such as pâtés, crépinettes, and stuffed cabbage to ensure they hold together during cooking. In anatomical terms, this is the omentum—the fold of the peritoneum that surrounds the intestines and connects the spleen and the stomach. Caul fat must be prepared before use (see technique p. 54).

FARCE: Also known as forcemeat, the word farce comes from the French verb *farcir* (to stuff). Farce is the foundation of many charcuterie staples, used to fill sausages, pâtés, terrines, savory pies, and more. It is traditionally made by mixing ground or pureed meat or fish with seasonings and sometimes a binding agent and/or additional fat. There are four categories of farce: rustic (or country); straight; gratin (in which some or all of the meat is previously cooked); and mousseline (the smoothest of all, made by pureeing the ingredients with egg whites and cream). For proper texture and hygiene, the ingredients should be kept as cold as possible when making the farce.

INTERIOR GARNISHES (*marquants*): Ingredients mixed with the farce in pâtés, terrines, and savory pies that add flavor, texture, and visual contrast.

LARD (*saindoux*): Rendered (melted and clarified) pork fat from different parts of the pig. The finest lard, known as leaf fat (see below), comes from the kidney region, as opposed to back and belly fat (see below).

***LARDO*:** A classic of Italian charcuterie (*salumi*) made by salting, seasoning, and dry-curing pork fatback. The most celebrated is *Lardo di Colonnata*.

LEAF FAT (*panne*): Also known as leaf lard, this is considered the pig's most noble fat and is the highest grade of lard you can buy. Rendered from the flare fat—the fat surrounding the kidneys—it has a neutral flavor and uniform white color.

PORK BELLY FAT (*mouille*): A cut of fat from the tougher outer layer and tail end of the pork belly, the *mouille* has a firm texture that does not melt easily. French charcutiers use this fat to make certain pâtés. Fatback is a good substitute.

PORK FATBACK (*lard gras or gras dur*): Also known as back fat, this layer of firm-textured fat is found on either side of the backbone of mature pigs. Fatback is essential to the flavor and texture of many charcuterie recipes.

PORK RIND (*couenne*): Also known as pork skin, it is composed of two layers—the dermis and epidermis. It has a neutral taste and is mainly used in charcuterie for its gelatin-rich properties.

TALLOW (*suif*): The fat rendered from beef and mutton fat, especially from suet, the solid fat surrounding the kidneys of cows, sheep, and other ruminants. In the UK, rendered beef fat is known as dripping.

MEAT CUTS

FRANCE

Pork

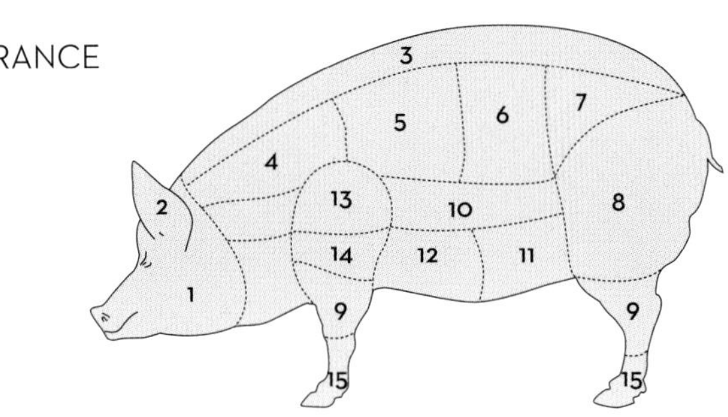

1. Tête **2.** Oreille **3.** Lard gras / gras dur / barde
4. Échine **5.** Carré **6.** Milieu de filet **7.** Pointe de filet
8. Jambon **9.** Jarret **10.** Travers **11.** Poitrine **12.** Plat de côtes
13. Palette **14.** Épaule **15.** Pieds

Lamb

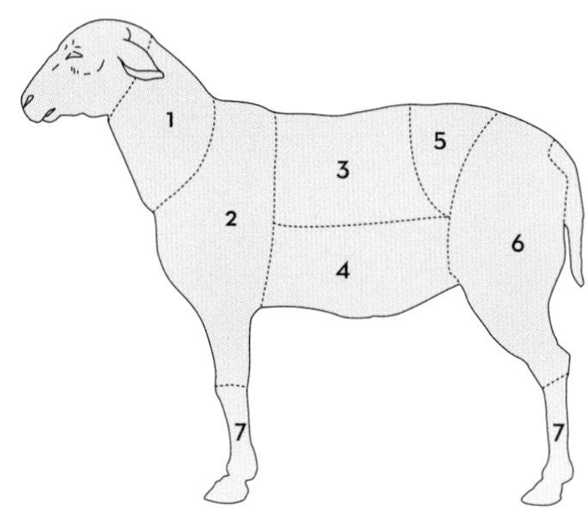

1. Collet **2.** Épaule **3.** Carré **4.** Poitrine
5. Selle **6.** Gigot **7.** Pieds

USA

Pork

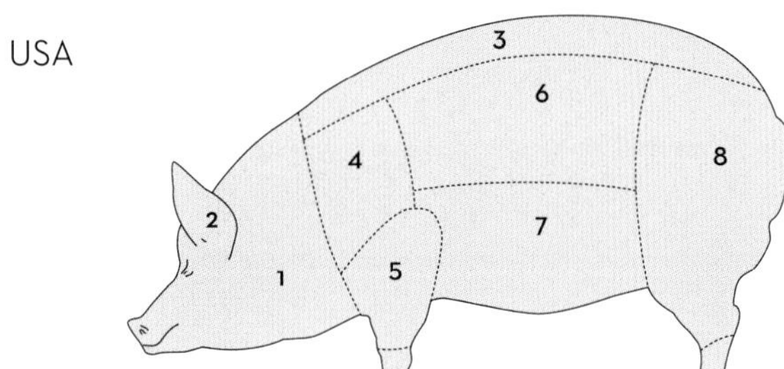

1. Head **2.** Ear **3.** Fatback **4.** Shoulder Butt
5. Picnic Shoulder **6.** Loin **7.** Spare Ribs/Belly
8. Ham **9.** Trotters

Lamb

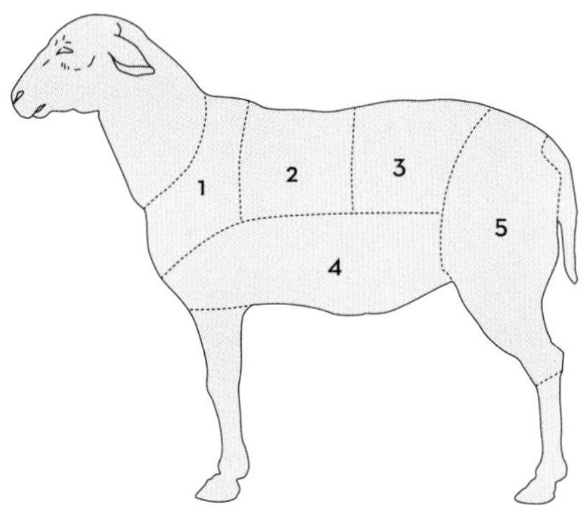

1. Shoulder **2.** Rack **3.** Loin
4. Foreshank and Breast **5.** Leg

UK

Pork

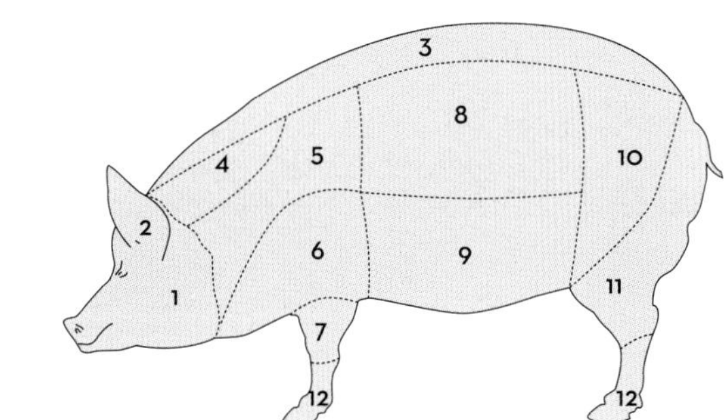

1. Head **2.** Ear **3.** Fatback **4.** Spare Rib **5.** Blade **6.** Hand
7. Hock **8.** Loin **9.** Belly **10.** Chump **11.** Leg **12.** Trotters

Lamb

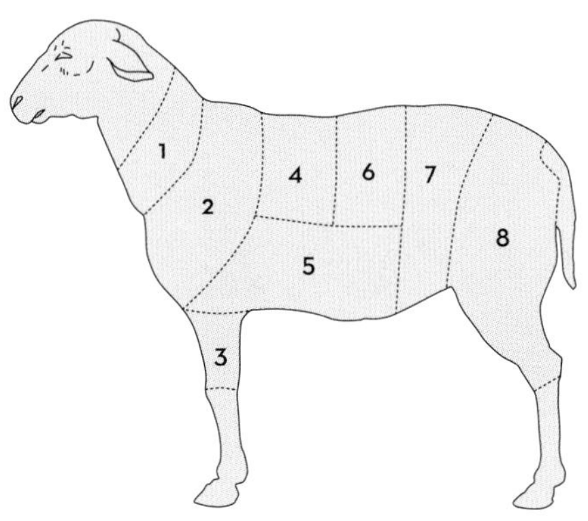

1. Scrag **2.** Shoulder **3.** Shank **4.** Best end of neck
5. Breast **6.** Loin **7.** Chump **8.** Leg

Veal

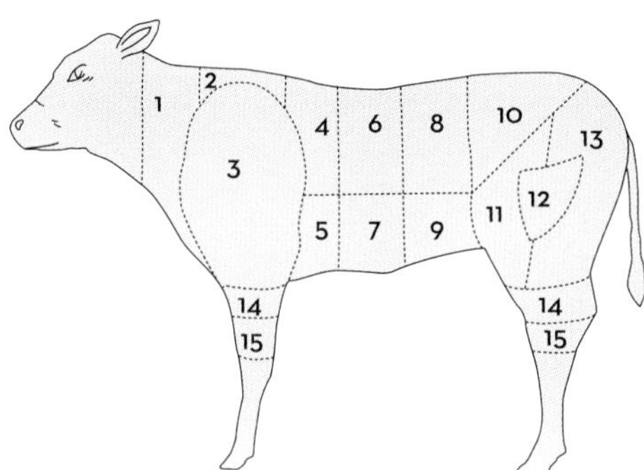

1. Collier **2.** Côtes découvertes **3.** Épaule **4.** Côtes secondes **5.** Poitrine **6.** Côtes premières **7.** Tendron **8.** Longe **9.** Flanchet **10.** Quasi **11.** Noix patissière **12.** Noix **13.** Sous-noix **14.** Jarret **15.** Crosse

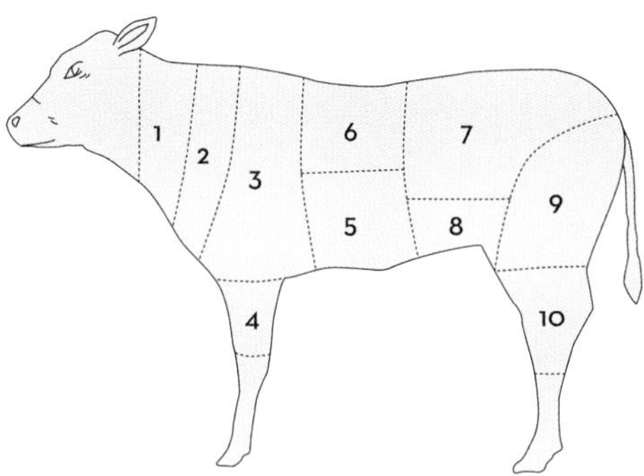

1. Neck **2.** Chuck **3.** Shoulder **4.** Fore Shank **5.** Breast **6.** Ribs **7.** Loin **8.** Flank **9.** Leg **10.** Hind Shank

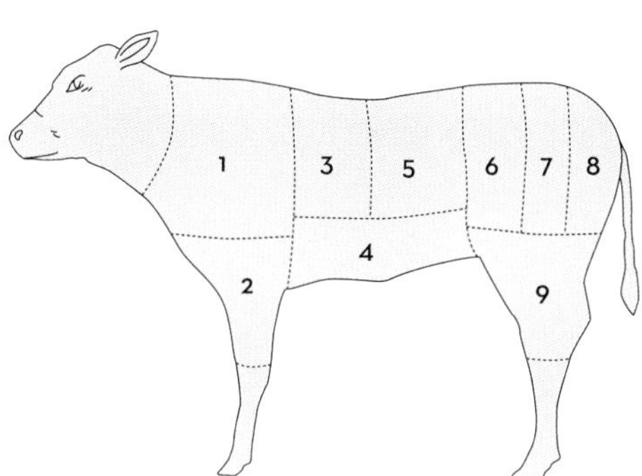

1. Shoulder **2.** Fore Shank **3.** Best End **4.** Breast **5.** Loin **6.** Rump **7.** Silverside **8.** Topside **9.** Hind Shank

Beef

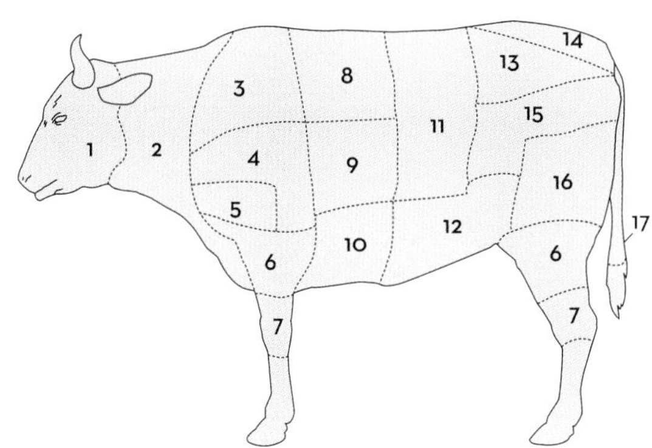

1. Joue **2.** Collier **3.** Paleron **4.** Macreuse **5.** Veine grasse **6.** Gîte **7.** Crosse **8.** Côtes couvertes **9.** Plat de côtes **10.** Poitrine **11.** Filet and aloyau **12.** Flanchet **13.** Culotte **14.** Rumsteck **15.** Tranche **16.** Gîte à la noix **17.** Queue de bœuf

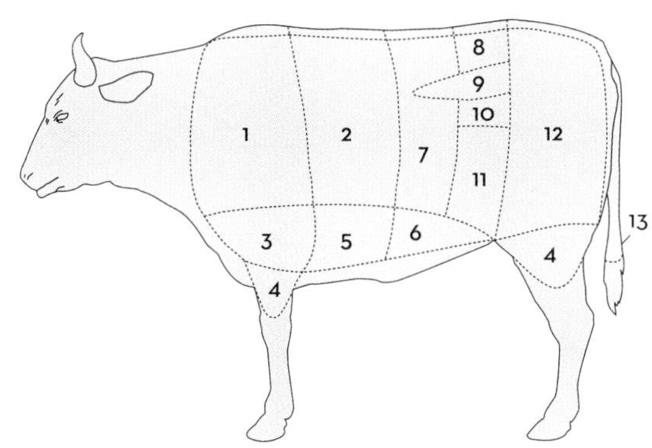

1. Chuck **2.** Rib **3.** Brisket **4.** Shank **5.** Plate **6.** Flank **7.** Short Loin **8.** Sirloin **9.** Tenderloin **10.** Top Sirloin **11.** Bottom Sirloin **12.** Round **13.** Oxtail

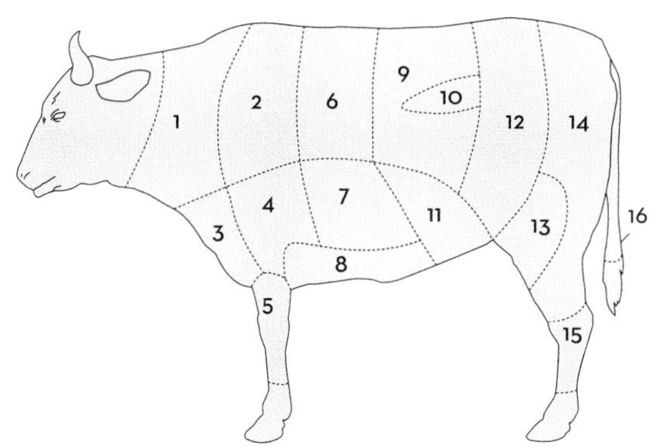

1. Neck **2.** Chuck and Blade **3.** Clod **4.** Thick Rib **5.** Shin **6.** Fore Rib **7.** Thin Rib **8.** Brisket **9.** Sirloin **10.** Fillet **11.** Thin Flank **12.** Rump **13.** Thick Flank **14.** Topside and Silverside **15.** Leg **16.** Oxtail

EQUIPMENT

1. Mandoline
2. Serrated knife
3. Large chef's knife
4. Small chef's knife
5. Paring knife
6. Swivel vegetable peeler
7. Y-peeler or Y-shaped peeler

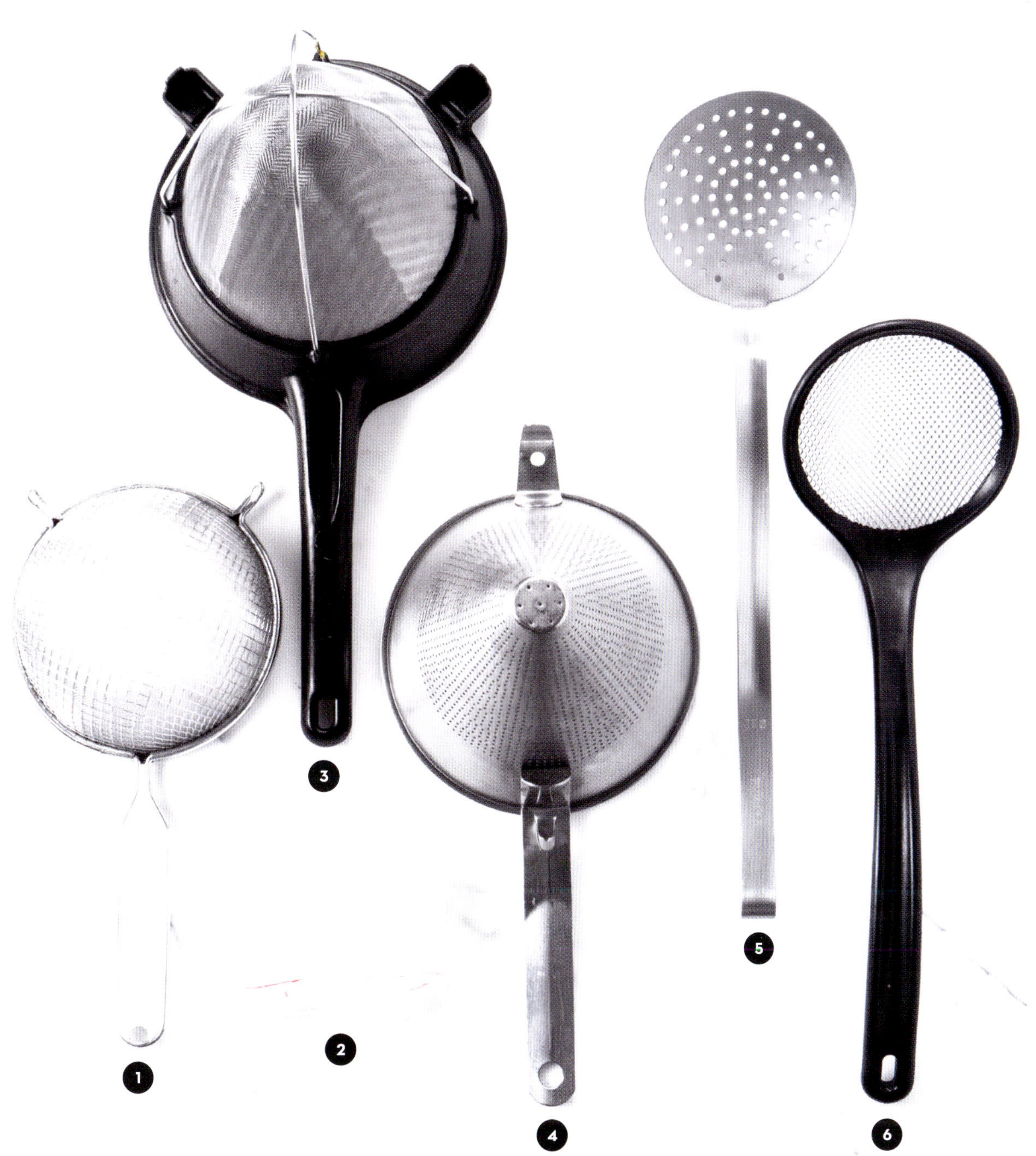

1. Strainer
2. Butter muslin
3. Fine-mesh sieve or strainer
4. China cap or conical sieve
5. Stainless steel skimmer
6. Nylon skimmer

1. Hinged baking ring for pâté en croûte
2. Hinged rectangular mold for pâté en croûte
3. Quenelle spoons
4. Oval cookie cutters
5. Round cookie cutters
6. Porcelain terrine molds

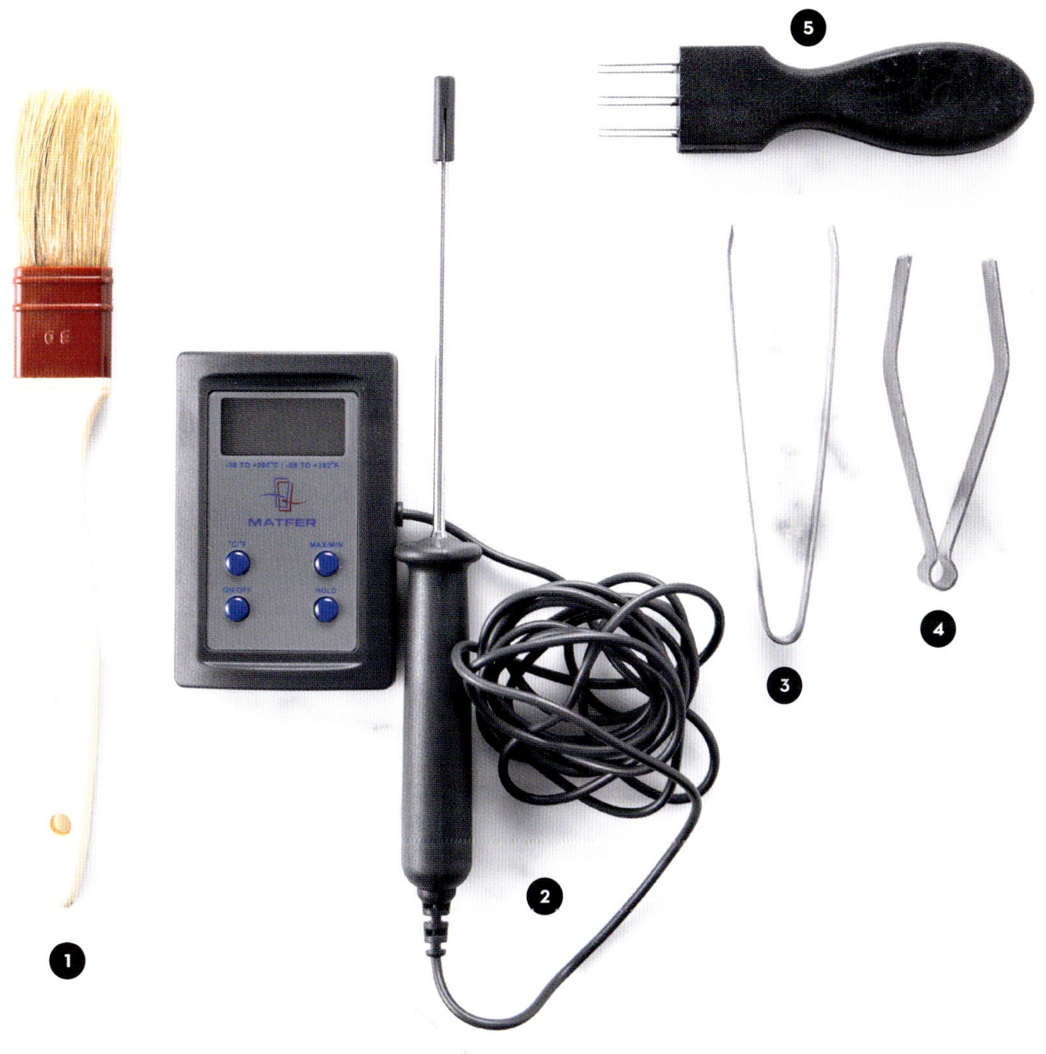

1. Pastry brush
2. Digital instant-read thermometer
3. Fish boning tweezers
4. Pie crimper
5. Sausage pricker

1. Stainless steel bowl
2. Blood sausage funnel
3. Butcher's twine
4. Sausage pricker

Electrical Appliances

1. Meat grinder
2. Assorted grinder plates

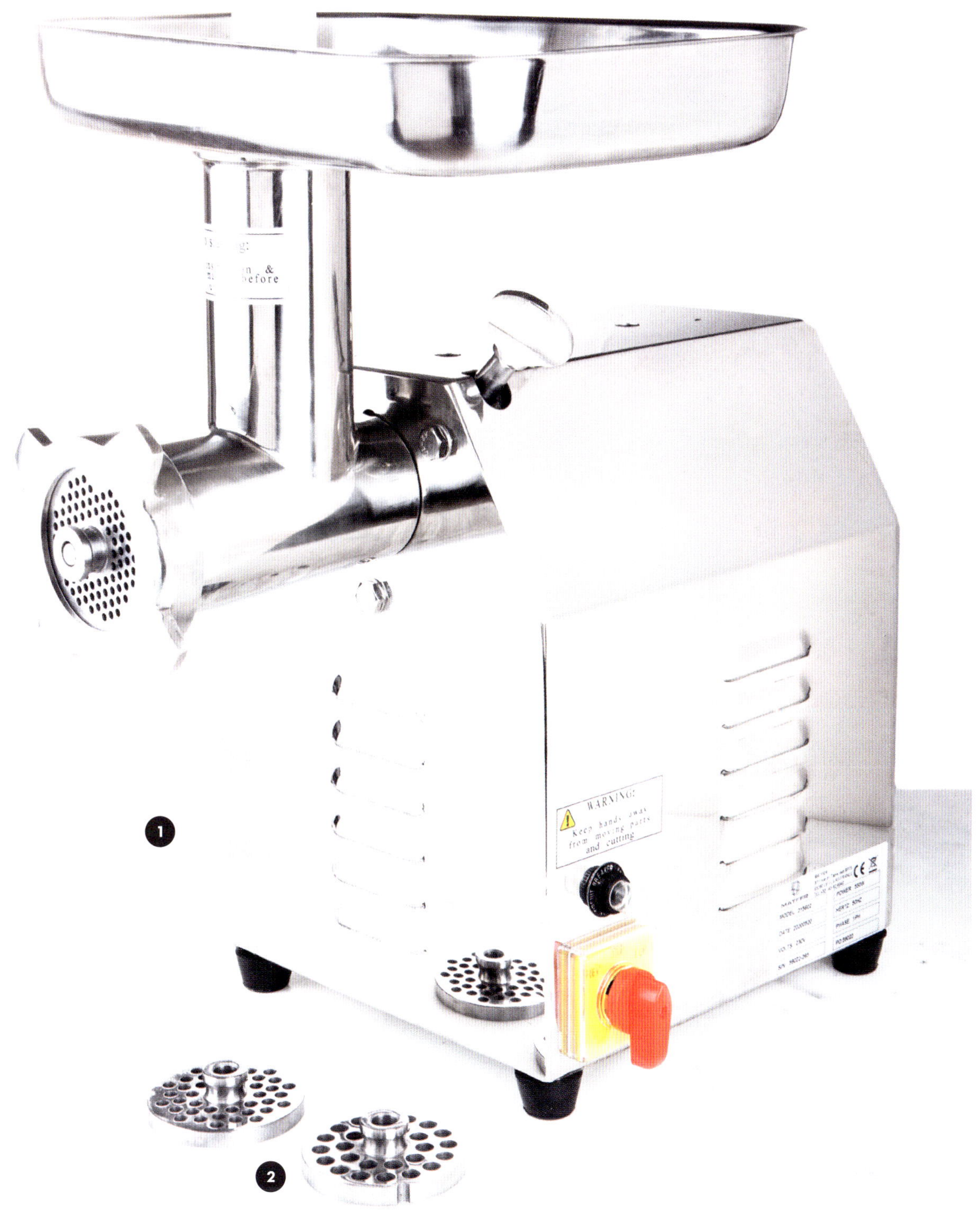
WARNING:
Keep hands away
from moving parts
and cutting
1
2

1.
Hand-operated sausage stuffer

2.
Assorted sausage stuffer filling tubes

3.
Crank / handle

1.
Sous vide vacuum sealer machine

2.
Sous vide vacuum bags

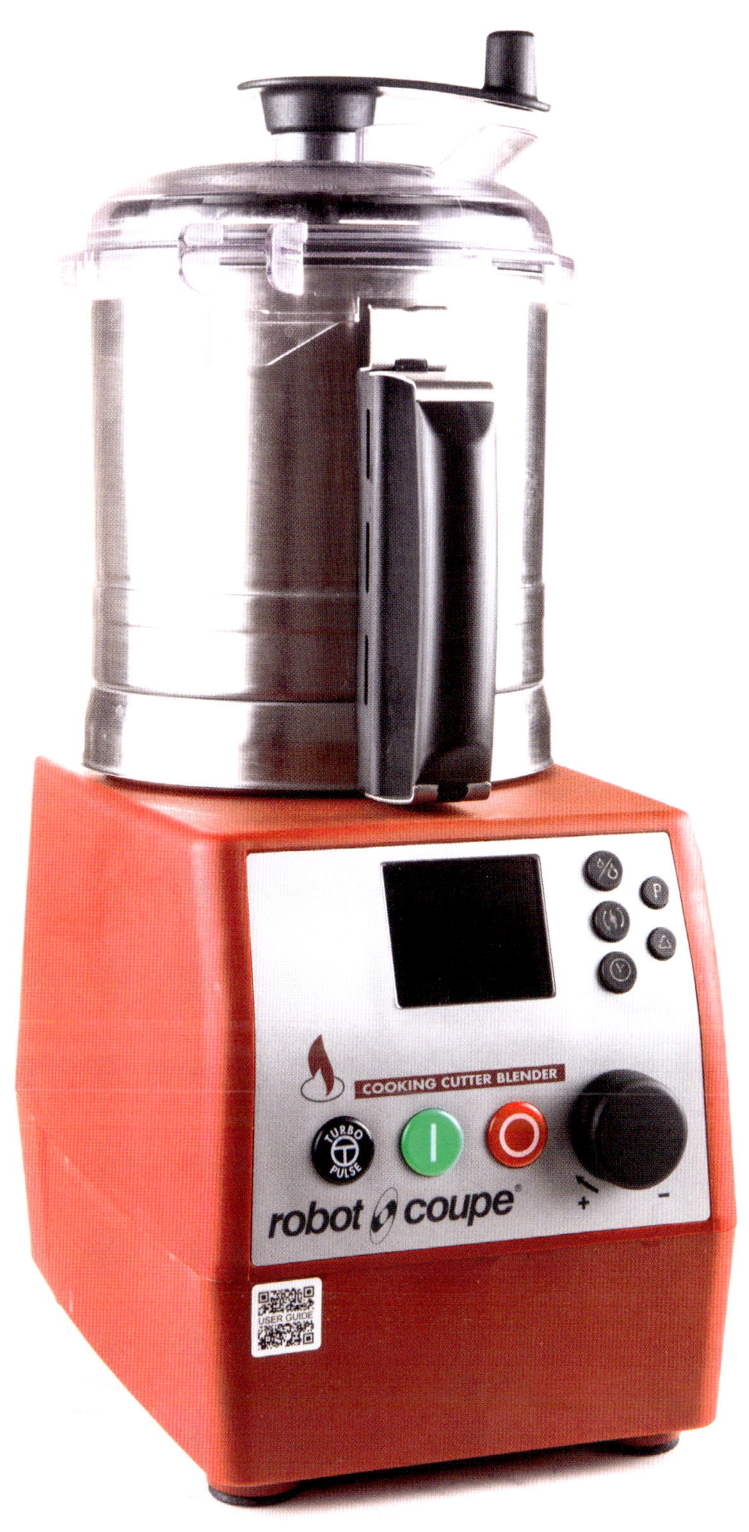

Food processor

TECHNIQUES

CUTTING AND CLEANING

Brunoise Cut

Ingredients
Carrots, or other firm vegetables

Equipment
Chef's knife
Mandoline

1 • Wash and peel the carrots. Cut them lengthwise into pieces, trimming the ends and sides flat. Cut into thin slices using the mandoline.

2 • Cut the slices into sticks about 1/16 in. (2 mm) wide.

3 • Cut the sticks into 1/16-in. (2-mm) cubes.

Slicing Onions

Ingredients
Onions

Equipment
Chef's knife

1 • Peel the onions and cut them in half lengthwise.

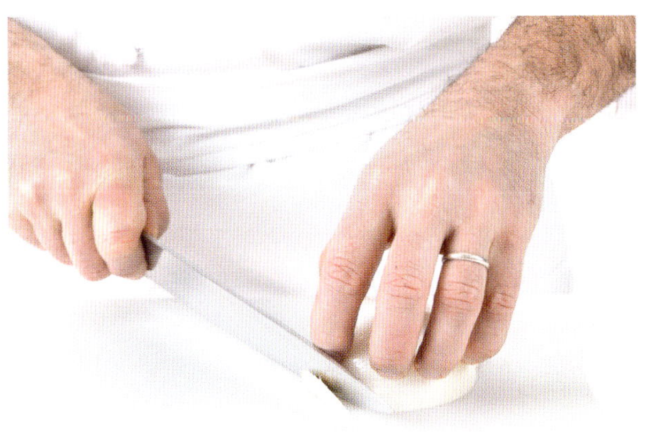

2 • Place cut side down and trim off the base.

3 • Cut each half into thin slices about ⅛ in. (2–3 mm) thick.

Finely Chopping Shallots or Onions

Ingredients
Shallots or onions

Equipment
Paring knife

1 • Peel the shallots or onions, and cut them in half lengthwise.

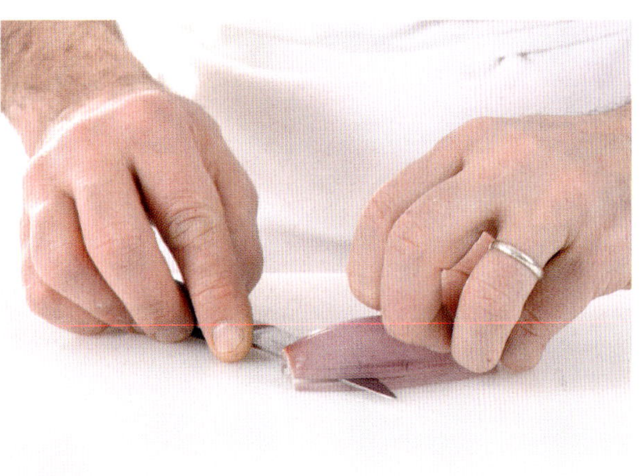

2 • Place cut side down and hold the base with your fingers bent under. With the knife parallel to the cutting board, make several horizontal cuts from the tip, stopping just short of the base.

3 • Continue by making several vertical cuts lengthwise.

4 • Make crosswise cuts close together, parallel to your fingers, to chop finely.

Cutting Meat into Strips and Cubes

Ingredients
Poultry breast, skinned and boned

Equipment
Chef's knife

1 • Cut the poultry breast horizontally into 2 even pieces, to reduce the thickness.

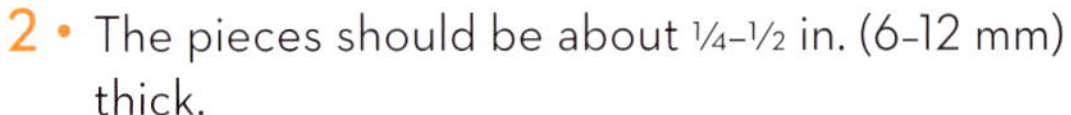

2 • The pieces should be about ¼–½ in. (6–12 mm) thick.

3 • Slice the pieces into strips measuring ¼–½ in. (6–12 mm) in width.

4 • Cut the strips crosswise into ¼–½-in. (6–12-mm) cubes.

Shredding Meat or Fish

Ingredients
Cooked meat or fish

Equipment
1 pair disposable gloves

CHEFS' NOTES

You can only shred meats or fish whose fibers separate like "threads" after cooking, such as duck confit, braised beef, or chicken.

1 • After slowly cooking the meat or fish in stock or another liquid until it is very tender, transfer it to a shallow dish.

2 • Wearing disposable gloves, pull the pieces of meat or fish apart while they are still warm.

3 • Continue shredding until the pieces are very fine.

Filleting, Deboning, and Skinning Fish

Ingredients

Round fish (such as salmon), gutted by your fishmonger

Equipment

Chef's knife

Fillet knife

Fish boning tweezers

1 • Using the chef's knife, remove the ventral (pelvic and anal) fins by carefully cutting around them.

2 • Remove the dorsal fin in the same way, using the chef's knife.

3 • Using the fillet knife, make a cut along the entire backbone.

Filleting, Deboning, and Skinning Fish (continued)

4 • Gradually lift the fillet, keeping the blade of the knife flat against the backbone.

5 • To remove the backbone, work the blade of the knife underneath the bone, lifting it with your thumb as it releases.

6 • Trim the fillets on both sides to remove the fatty parts and obtain clean edges.

7 • Using the tweezers, pull out the pin bones. Run your hand over the flesh to locate them.

8 • Lay the fillet flat. Starting at the tail end, begin cutting with the chef's knife between the skin and the flesh.

9 • Firmly hold onto the skin at the tail end and continue cutting.

10 • Cut away any fatty parts left on the flesh. Remove the other fillet in the same way.

Deveining Foie Gras

Ingredients

1 whole foie gras

Optional seasonings of your choice (such as salt, pepper, alcohol, etc.)

Equipment

Paring knife

1 • Gently separate the two lobes.

CHEFS' NOTES

Removing all the veins ensures the smoothest possible results. Don't worry about mangling the foie, as the lobes can be reshaped once you've finished.

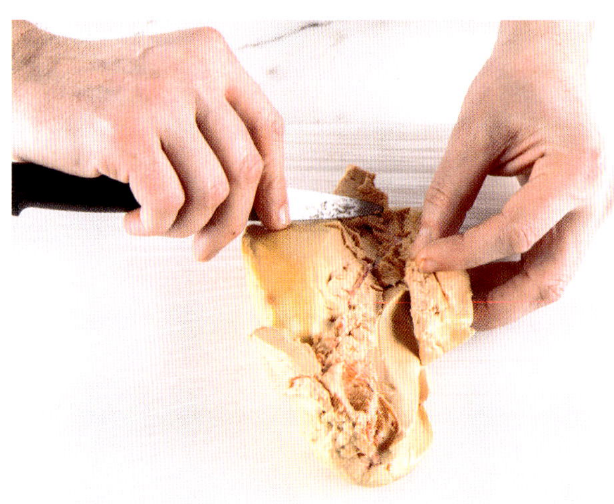

2 • Using the tip of the paring knife, start to detach the central vein from the top of the large lobe.

3 • Separate the entire vein network from the lobe. Feel free to use your fingers to do this and to cut the lobe if necessary (see Chefs' Notes).

4 • Once the vein is detached, gently pull to remove it completely, making sure no part of the vein remains. Do the same for the lower vein. Repeat with the other lobe.

5 • If you wish, season the foie gras on all sides with your chosen seasonings before the next step.

6 • Gather the two lobes together to reform the foie gras. Cover in plastic wrap to keep its shape.

Cleaning Veal Sweetbreads

Ingredients
Veal sweetbreads

Soaking time
½–1 hour

Equipment
2 large bowls
Chef's knife

1 • Rinse the sweetbreads in a large bowl of water, then soak them in a separate bowl filled with ice water for ½–1 hour, to remove all traces of blood.

CHEFS' NOTES

To cook the sweetbreads, simply place them in a large saucepan of cold salted water, bring to a boil, and let simmer for 2 minutes. Drain the sweetbreads and plunge them into a bowl of ice water to stop the cooking.

2 • Place on paper towel and pat dry.

3 • Using the chef's knife, gently cut along the veins to remove them.

4 • Cut off the fat.

5 • Gently remove the membrane.

Cleaning Natural Casings

Ingredients
Natural hog or sheep casing

Equipment
2 large bowls

1 • Check the entire length of the casing to ensure that there are no holes.

2 • Completely submerge the casing in a large bowl filled with water.

3 • Rinse the casing by passing it between your fingers, then immerse it in a separate bowl filled with clean water.

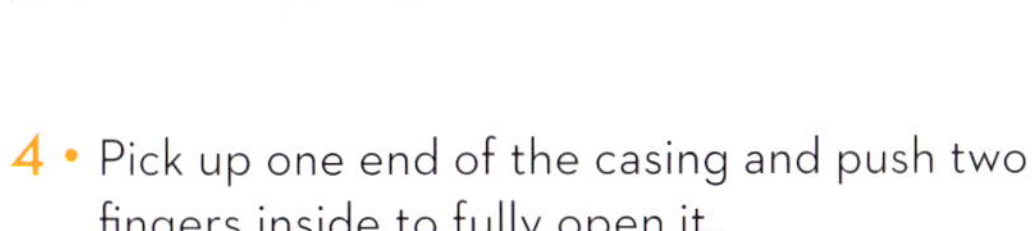

4 • Pick up one end of the casing and push two fingers inside to fully open it.

5 • Submerge the open end so that a little water gets inside.

6 • This will create a small pocket of water in the casing.

7 • Hold the casing on either side of this water pocket and push the water all the way through the casing to clean the inside.

Preparing Caul Fat

Ingredients
Caul fat
Salt

Equipment
Large bowl

1 • Rinse the caul fat thoroughly in a bowl of water.

2 • Lift the caul fat out of the water and submerge it again several times to ensure it is thoroughly cleaned.

3 • Wring it between your hands, squeezing it well to remove all the water.

4 • Lay the caul fat flat on a clean work surface.

5 • Sprinkle it with salt.

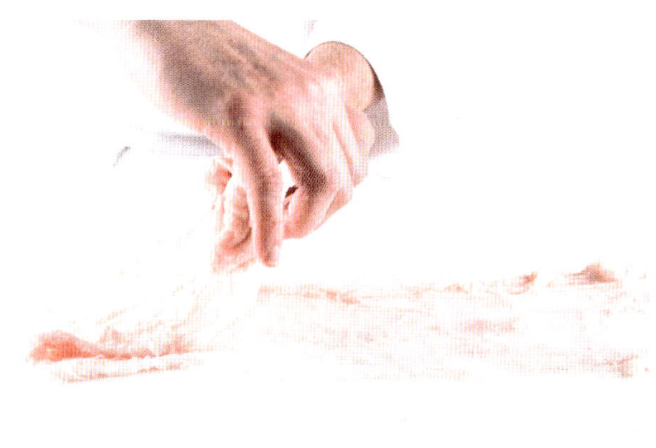

6 • Carefully fold the caul fat.

7 • You should end up with a compact parcel.
Cover with plastic wrap and chill until using.

BASE RECIPES

Quick Puff Pastry

Makes 1½ lb. (675 g)

Active time
30 minutes

Chilling time
1¾ hours

Storage
2 days, well wrapped (but best used on day it is made)

Ingredients

2 cups (9 oz./250 g) strong white bread flour, sifted

1 tsp (5 g) salt

½ cup (125 ml) water

1¾ sticks (7 oz./200 g) butter, well chilled, cut into 1-in. (2-cm) dice

1 • Shape the flour into a mound on a cool work surface and make a well in the center. Dissolve the salt in the water and pour it into the well. Add the diced butter.

2 • Working with your fingertips, draw the flour gradually into the well. Continue working with a pastry scraper to combine the ingredients into a rough dough. The pieces of butter should marble the dough and they should still be cold. Shape the dough into a ball.

3 • Lightly dust the work surface with flour and roll the dough into a rectangle.

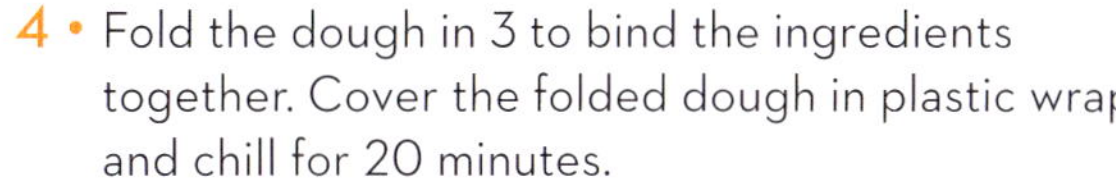

4 • Fold the dough in 3 to bind the ingredients together. Cover the folded dough in plastic wrap and chill for 20 minutes.

5 • Remove from the refrigerator and begin rolling out the dough.

6 • Roll the dough into a rectangle measuring 10 × 28 in. (25 × 70 cm).

Quick Puff Pastry (continued)

7 • Fold the shorter ends of the dough toward the center, one-third of the way down from the top and two-thirds up from the bottom, then fold the dough in half (double turn).

8 • The dough now has 4 folds. Cover the dough in plastic wrap and chill for 30–40 minutes. Repeat steps 5–8 twice more. Cover in plastic wrap and chill for 30–40 minutes.

9 • Give the dough one final single turn (folding it in 3) before using.

CHEFS' NOTES

• Mark the dough lightly with your finger after each turn, so you can keep track of how many turns you have made.

• Quick puff pastry is ideal to make when time is short. It can keep for up to 2 days, but is best used soon after it is made.

Pastry for Pâté en Croûte

Makes 4 lb. (1.8 kg)

Active time
15 minutes

Chilling time
12 hours

Storage
4 days in the refrigerator

Equipment
Bowl scraper

Ingredients
- 5⅔ cups (1½ lb./700 g) all-purpose flour
- 2 cups (10½ oz./300 g) potato starch
- 4 sticks plus 3 tbsp (1 lb. 2 oz./500 g) butter, well chilled
- 4 tsp (20 g) salt
- ⅓ cup (3½ oz./100 g) egg yolk (about 5 yolks)
- ⅔ cup (160 ml) water
- 4 tsp (20 ml) white vinegar

1 • Combine the flour and potato starch on a work surface.

CHEFS' NOTES

Take care not to overwork the dough as it will become too elastic and lose its shape while baking.

2 • Dice the butter and add with the salt.

3 • Start rubbing the ingredients together with your hands.

4 • Continue rubbing with your fingertips until the mixture has the texture of coarse crumbs.

5 • Make a well in the center.

6 • Place the egg yolks, water, and vinegar into the well.

↪

Pastry for Pâté en Croûte (continued)

7 • Working with your fingertips, gradually draw the flour into the well so it combines with the egg yolks, water, and vinegar and forms into a dough.

8 • Push down on the dough with the heel of your hand, smearing it against the work surface until smooth (*fraisage*).

9 • Shape the dough into a square or disk.

10 • Cover with plastic wrap and chill for 12 hours before using.

Brine

Makes 6¾ cups (1.6 liters)

Active time
15 minutes

Ingredients
4 cups (1 liter) still mineral water, at 50°F (10°C)
1⅓ cups (320 ml) decoction (see technique p. 68), cooled to 50°F (10°C)
8¾ oz. (245 g) grey sea salt
2 oz. (55 g) dextrose
1⁄10 oz. (3 g) ascorbic acid

Equipment
Large bowl
Whisk

1 • Pour the water and decoction into a large bowl.

2 • Sprinkle in the remaining ingredients.

3 • Mix using the whisk to dissolve completely. Cover with plastic wrap and chill until using (for brining large pieces of meat such as knuckles (*jarrets*), shoulders (*palettes*), tongues (*langues*), heads (*têtes*), etc.).

Decoction

Makes 5 cups (1.2 liters)

Active time
10 minutes

Cooking time
1 hour

Storage
30 days in the refrigerator

Equipment
Fine-mesh sieve

Ingredients
4 cups (1 liter) water
1½ cups (375 ml) white wine
12 g black peppercorns
12 juniper berries
⅕ oz. (4 g) fresh sage
⅕ oz. (4 g) fresh savory
⅕ oz. (4 g) garlic
4 bay leaves
¼ oz. (8 g) fresh thyme
2 whole cloves
9 oz. (250 g) onion, charred (see Chefs' Notes)
4½ oz. (125 g) celery
⅓ oz. (10 g) dried hibiscus flowers
1 tsp (3 g) beet powder

1 • Pour the water and white wine into a large saucepan.

CHEFS' NOTES

To prepare the charred onion, wash and cut the onion in half, leaving the skin on. Place a square of aluminum foil in a skillet and heat. Place the onion halves cut side down on the foil and let cook until charred.

2 • Add all the remaining ingredients and bring to a boil.

3 • Let simmer and infuse over low heat for 1 hour.

4 • Remove from the heat, cover the pan with plastic wrap, and let cool completely.

5 • Strain through the fine-mesh sieve into a bowl. Chill in a covered container until using.

Jellied Broth

Makes 3 qt. (3 liters)

Active time
30 minutes

Soaking time
1 hour

Cooking time
8½ hours

Storage
10 days in the refrigerator

Equipment
Chef's knife
Skimmer
Instant-read thermometer
Fine-mesh sieve
Muslin

Ingredients
3½ lb. (1.5 kg) pork rind (*couenne de porc*)
Vinegar
5 oz. (150 g) carrots
5 oz. (150 g) leek
5 oz. (150 g) onion
2 unpeeled cloves garlic
3 qt. (3 liters) water
⅔ oz. (18 g) coarse grey sea salt
⅓ oz. (10 g) fresh thyme
2 bay leaves
1 whole clove
5 peppercorns

1 • Place the pork rind on a work surface, rind side down, and roll up lengthwise.

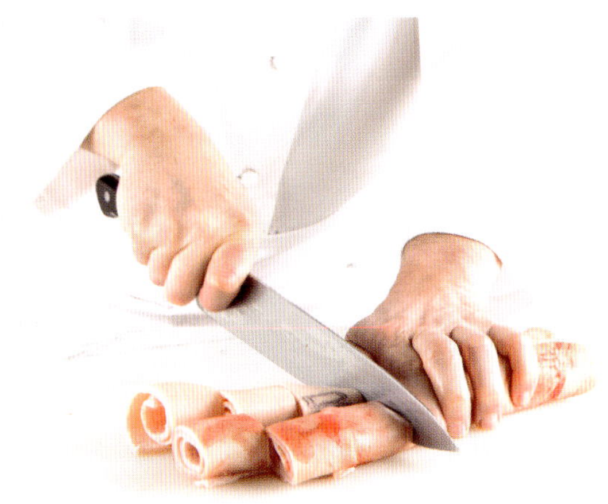

2 • Cut into approximately 2-in. (5-cm) pieces.

3 • Place in a saucepan and cover with cold water, measuring the quantity of water. Add vinegar equal to 5% of the volume of water. Let soak for 1 hour at room temperature.

4 • Preheat the oven to 350°F (180°C/Gas Mark 4). Wash the carrots and leek. Slice the roots off the leek, halve it lengthwise, and cut into approximately ½-in. (1-cm) pieces.

5 • Peel the carrots and onion. Cut the carrots diagonally into approximately ½-in. (1-cm) pieces and quarter the onions. Cut the unpeeled garlic cloves in half. Place in a baking dish and roast for 20 minutes, until well browned (alternatively, use a skillet).

6 • Drain the pork rind and place in a clean saucepan with the 3 qt. (3 liters) water and sea salt.
Bring to a boil, skimming off any foam as it rises to the surface. Add the herbs, clove, peppercorns, and roasted vegetables.

↪

Jellied Broth (continued)

7 • Add the leeks and bring back to a boil.

8 • Simmer, covered (see step 9), over low heat (at about 185°F/85°C) for 8 hours.

9 • You can cover the saucepan with plastic wrap or a tight-fitting lid.

10 • Strain through the fine-mesh sieve, then through muslin. Let cool, then press plastic wrap over the surface and store in the refrigerator for up to 10 days.

CHEFS' NOTES

This broth can also be stored in the freezer for up to 6 months in a sealed freezer bag.

Basic Broth

Makes 5 qt. (5 liters)

Active time
30 minutes

Soaking time
1 hour

Cooking time
6 hours

Storage
10 days in the refrigerator

Equipment
Chef's knife
Skimmer
Instant-read thermometer
Fine-mesh sieve
Muslin

Ingredients
3½ lb. (1.5 kg) pork rind (*couenne de porc*)
White vinegar
4½ oz. (125 g) onion
4½ oz. (125 g) carrot
3½ oz. (100 g) leek
5 oz. (150 g) fennel
5 oz. (150 g) celery
1½ oz. (40 g) head garlic
3½ lb. (1.5 kg) pork bones
6 qt. (6 liters) water
1 oz. (25 g) coarse grey sea salt
½ oz. (15 g) fresh thyme
2 bay leaves
2 whole cloves
10 peppercorns
1½ cups (375 ml) white wine

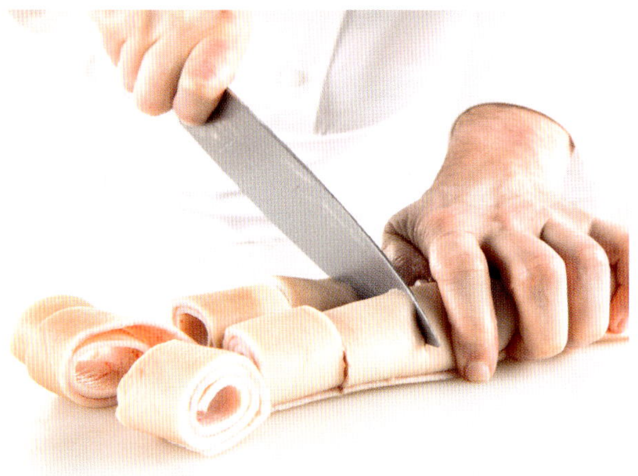

1 • Roll up the pork rind and cut into 2-in. (5-cm) slices. Place in a bowl and cover with cold water, measuring the quantity of water. Add white vinegar equal to 5% of the volume of water. Let soak for 1 hour at room temperature.

CHEFS' NOTES

This broth can also be stored in the freezer for up to 6 months in a sealed freezer bag.

2 • Wash the vegetables. Quarter the unpeeled onion and cut the other vegetables into large pieces.

3 • Separate and peel the garlic cloves, and remove the germs. Crush with the flat side of the chef's knife.

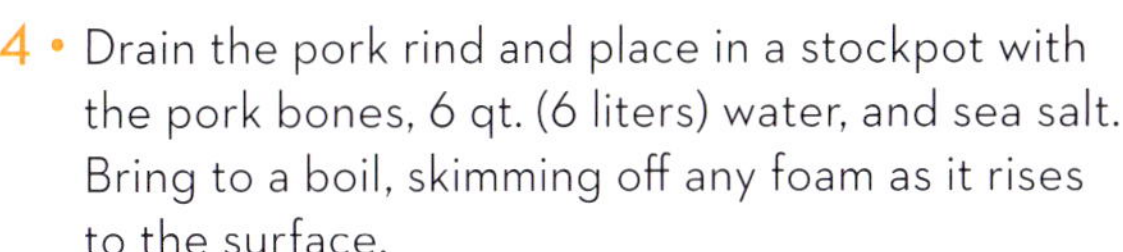

4 • Drain the pork rind and place in a stockpot with the pork bones, 6 qt. (6 liters) water, and sea salt. Bring to a boil, skimming off any foam as it rises to the surface.

5 • Add the vegetables, garlic, herbs, cloves, peppercorns, and white wine. Bring back to a boil. Simmer over low heat (at about 185°F/85°C) for 6 hours.

6 • Strain through the fine-mesh sieve, then through muslin. Cool quickly by pouring into a larger container. Press plastic wrap over the surface and store in the refrigerator for up to 10 days.

Clarifying Broth

Makes 4 cups (1 liter)

Active time
10 minutes

Cooking time
1 hour

Storage
20 days in the refrigerator

Equipment
Chef's knife
Ladle
Fine-mesh sieve lined with muslin

Ingredients
1½ oz. (40 g) onion
1 clove garlic
1½ oz. (40 g) carrot
1½ oz. (40 g) leek
¾ oz. (20 g) celery
7 oz. (200 g) poultry breast
1 egg white
4 cups (1 liter) cold chicken stock

1 • Wash, peel (as necessary), and cut the onion, garlic, carrot, leek, and celery into brunoise (see technique p. 38).

2 • Dice the poultry breast very finely.

3 • Place the vegetables and poultry breast in a bowl and add the egg white. Using a spatula, stir to combine.

4 • Pour the stock into a large saucepan, add the contents of the bowl, and bring to a boil over low heat, stirring occasionally. As soon as the liquid starts to boil, reduce the heat to very low and cook for 1 hour without stirring.

5 • Remove from the heat. Using the ladle, pour into the muslin-lined sieve set over a bowl to obtain a clear consommé.

Salmon Mousseline Farce

Makes 1 lb. 3 oz. (550 g)

Active time
20 minutes

Freezing time
10 minutes

Storage
2 days in the refrigerator

Equipment
Chef's knife
Food processor
Fine-mesh drum sieve

Ingredients

9 oz. (250 g) salmon fillet, skinned and pin boned (see technique p. 45)

1 cup (250 ml) heavy cream, min. 35% fat, well chilled

1½ tsp (8 g) fine salt

Scant ½ tsp (1 g) ground white pepper

1 tsp (5 g) lightly beaten egg

1 • Cut the salmon into ¾-in. (2-cm) pieces and freeze for 10 minutes to firm up. Place the cream and the bowl of the food processor in the freezer, too.

2 • Place the salmon, salt, and pepper in the food processor and process to a smooth paste.

3 • With the motor running, add the egg, then gradually add the cream. Process until smooth, taking care not to overheat the farce.

CHEFS' NOTES

Be sure to keep the mixture cold as you work, returning it to the refrigerator for a few minutes at a time, as needed, in a sealed freezer bag.

4 • For best results, pass the farce through the fine-mesh sieve.

Sausage Meat

Makes 1 lb. 14 oz. (850 g)

Active time
10 minutes

Chilling time
24 hours

Storage
3 days in the refrigerator

Equipment
Chef's knife
Meat grinder + plate with ¼-in. (6-mm) holes
Disposable gloves

Ingredients
1¼ lb. (600 g) lean pork shoulder (*épaule de porc maigre*)
7 oz. (200 g) hard pork fatback (*gras dur de porc*)
2½ tsp (12 g) salt
1 tsp (2.5 g) ground white pepper
3½ tbsp (50 ml) cold water

1 • Cut the pork shoulder and fatback into approximately 1½-in. (4-cm) pieces.

CHEFS' NOTES

You can flavor the sausage meat with finely chopped parsley or garlic, for instance.

2 • Grind the meat through the meat grinder fitted with the plate with ¼-in. (6-mm) holes.

3 • Season with the salt and pepper.

4 • At first, mix with a spatula.

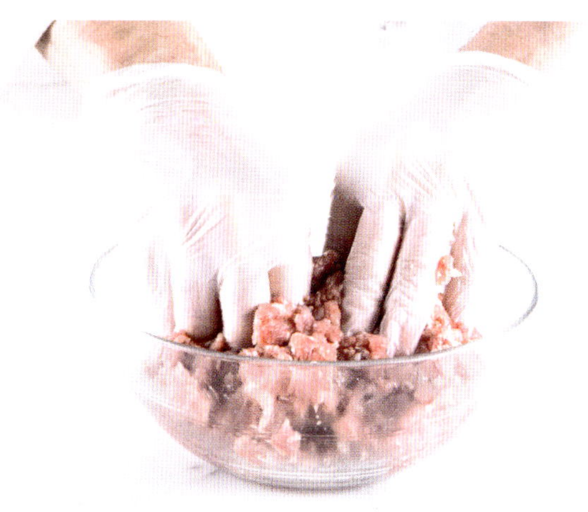

5 • Add the cold water and, wearing disposable gloves, mix well using your fingers to draw the collagen out of the meat. Press plastic wrap over the surface and chill for 24 hours before using.

Salmon Rillettes

Makes 2 lb. (900 g)

Active time
30 minutes

Cooking time
6–8 minutes

Storage
2 days in the refrigerator

Equipment
Chef's knife
Steamer basket

Ingredients
14 oz. (400 g) salmon fillet, skinned and pin boned (see technique p. 45)
7 oz. (200 g) smoked salmon
¼ bunch parsley
½ bunch chives
1¾ oz. (50 g) shallots
½ scallion
1 tsp (5 g) salt
Freshly ground pepper
1½ sticks (6 oz./180 g) butter, softened
3 tbsp (1¾ oz./50 g) wholegrain mustard (preferably Meaux)
¾ tsp (2 g) *piment d'Espelette*
Finely grated zest and juice of ½ lime

1 • Cut the salmon fillet into approximately 1¼-in. (3-cm) pieces.

2 • Place in the steamer basket and cover airtight with plastic wrap. Set the basket over a saucepan of boiling water and steam for 6–8 minutes.

3 • Cut the smoked salmon into approximately ¼-in. (5-mm) dice.

↪

Salmon Rillettes (continued)

4 • Finely chop the parsley and chives.

5 • Peel and finely chop the shallots.
Finely chop the scallion.

6 • Place the cooked salmon in a large bowl and break it into small pieces using a spatula.

7 • In a separate large bowl, combine the smoked salmon, shallots, scallion, and herbs.

8 • Add the cooked salmon and season with the salt and pepper. Using a spatula, work in the butter, followed by the mustard.

9 • Stir in the *piment d'Espelette* and lime zest and juice until well combined.

CHEFS' NOTES

Combining steamed and smoked salmon adds extra flavor and texture to these rillettes.

Pork Rillettes

Makes about 2¼ lb. (1 kg)

Active time
40 minutes

Cooking time
5 hours

Storage
20 days in the refrigerator

Equipment
Instant-read thermometer
Skimmer
Disposable gloves
Terrine mold

Ingredients
13 oz. (375 g) bone-in pork belly (*poitrine de porc*)
10½ oz. (300 g) bone-in pork shoulder (*épaule de porc*)
8 oz. (225 g) bone-in middle pork shoulder (*palette de porc*)
4 oz. (120 g) hard pork fatback (*gras dur de porc*)
⅔ cup (160 ml) water, divided
10½ oz. (300 g) lard
5 oz. (150 g) white onions
1½ cloves garlic
1½ bay leaves
1½ sprigs thyme
2½ tsp (12 g) Guérande sea salt
1 tsp (2.5 g) ground white pepper
1 tsp *piment d'Espelette*

1 • Remove the skin and bones (reserve the pork belly bones) and cut the meat into 1½-in. (4-cm) pieces. Cut the fatback into ½-in. (1-cm) dice and heat in a large saucepan with 3 tbsp (40 ml) water. Add the lard and heat until melted.

2 • Increase the heat and gradually add the meats. Cook until lightly browned, stirring often. When the juices are clear, lower the heat.

3 • Peel and finely chop the onions and garlic. Add to the saucepan with the bay leaves, thyme, salt, pork belly bones, and ½ cup (120 ml) water. Cook partially uncovered at 185°F (85°C) for 5 hours, without stirring.

CHEFS' NOTES

Avoid mixing the rillettes once they are in the terrine mold—this could make the fat rise to the top.

4 • Remove the bones. Using the skimmer, carefully transfer the meat to a roasting pan. Pour the pan juices into a tall container with straight sides and let sit until the fat rises to the top. Slowly pour just the fat into a saucepan and warm over medium heat.

5 • Wearing the gloves, shred the meat (see technique p. 44), then add the pan juices.

6 • Transfer to a large bowl and gradually pour in the warm fat, stirring continuously with a spatula. Add the pepper and *piment d'Espelette*, then adjust the seasonings if necessary. Transfer to the terrine mold, making sure the fat and meat are evenly distributed.

Pork Belly Rillons

Serves 8

Active time
30 minutes

Cooking time
8 hours

Chilling time
12 hours

Storage
5 days in the refrigerator

Equipment
Chef's knife
Sous vide bag + vacuum sealer machine
Instant-read thermometer

Ingredients
7 oz. (200 g) white onions
1⁄3 oz. (10 g) garlic
3 cups (750 ml) Vouvray white wine
2 sprigs fresh thyme
2 bay leaves
1 whole clove
4 1⁄2 lb. (2 kg) pork belly (*poitrine de porc*)
5 tsp (25 g) salt
2 tsp (5 g) ground pepper
1 1⁄4 tsp (5 g) sugar
3⁄4 tsp (2 g) quatre-épices spice mix
1 1⁄2 lb. (750 g) lard

1 • Peel and thinly slice the onions. Peel the garlic, remove the germs, and crush with the flat side of the chef's knife.

2 • Place the wine, onion, and garlic in a sauté pan and cook until tender and reduced. Remove from the heat and add the thyme, bay leaves, and clove. Let cool.

3 • Preheat the oven to 175°F (80°C/Gas on lowest setting). Using the chef's knife, cut the rind off the pork belly and remove the bones.

4 • Combine the salt, pepper, sugar, and quatre-épices and rub all over both sides of the pork belly.

5 • Place the pork belly in the sous vide bag with the cooked onions.

6 • Vacuum seal the bag, place in a baking dish, and bake for 8 hours. Let cool completely, then refrigerate for 12 hours in the bag with a weight on top to keep it flat.

↪

Pork Belly Rillons (continued)

7 • Remove the pork belly from the bag.

8 • Using paper towel, thoroughly pat the meat dry.

9 • Cut the pork belly into even 2 × 2¾-in. (5 × 7-cm) pieces.

10 • Heat the lard to between 330°F and 347°F (165°C and 175°C) in a large saucepan. Deep-fry the pork belly pieces for a few minutes, until golden brown. Drain on a rack or paper towel and serve hot, warm, or at room temperature.

Boudin Blanc

Makes 10

Active time
30 minutes

Chilling time
12 hours

Cooking time
20 minutes

Storage
4 days in the refrigerator

Equipment
Meat grinder + large plate
Food processor
Fine-mesh sieve
Instant-read thermometer
Manual sausage stuffer
Sausage pricker

Ingredients
14 oz. (400 g) pork belly (*poitrine de porc*)
3½ oz. (100 g) poultry breast
1½ tsp (7 g) fine salt
¾ tsp (2 g) ground white pepper
⅛ tsp (0.5 g) five-spice powder
1¼ oz. (35 g) white onion
2 cups (500 ml) whole milk
1 pinch (0.25 g) ground nutmeg
1 whole clove
1/20 (0.3 g) vanilla bean
1 bay leaf
2½ tbsp (25 g) all-purpose flour
3 eggs
2 tsp (10 ml) port wine
5 ft. (1.5 m) natural hog casing, 34/36 mm, cleaned
(see technique p. 52)

1 • Cut the meats into 1¼–1½-in. (3–4-cm) pieces and place in a large bowl with the salt, pepper, and five-spice powder. Using a spatula, stir to combine. Press plastic wrap over the surface and chill for 12 hours.

2 • The same day, peel and thinly slice the onion. Place in a bowl with the milk, nutmeg, clove, vanilla bean, and bay leaf. Cover with plastic wrap and chill for 12 hours.

3 • The next day, bring the infused milk to a boil in a saucepan. Remove from the heat and cover.

4 • Meanwhile, grind the seasoned meat through the meat grinder.

5 • Place the ground meat in the food processor. Add the flour and eggs and process to a smooth paste. Mix in the port wine.

6 • Strain the milk through the fine-mesh sieve and let cool to about 130°F (55°C). With the processor running, gradually pour the milk into the farce. Transfer to a bowl.

↪

Boudin Blanc (continued)

7 • Slide one end of the casing onto the filling tube of the sausage stuffer.

8 • Start cranking the stuffer with one hand, holding the casing in place with the other hand.
Fill a little over 1 in. (2.5 cm) of the casing with the farce, then tie a knot at the end.

9 • Continue filling until you have used up all the farce, then coil the boudin into a spiral.
Using the sausage pricker, pierce all over to eliminate air bubbles.

10 • Shape into individual boudins measuring 5–5 ½ in. (12–14 cm) in length, by pinching and twisting (see technique p. 110).
Tie a knot at the end. Place in a saucepan of water heated to 176°F (80°C), cover with plastic wrap, and cook for 20 minutes.

11 • Transfer the boudins to a bowl of ice water.
Let sit for 15 minutes, then drain.
Serve immediately or store in the refrigerator
covered in plastic wrap.

Blood Sausage

Makes 16

Active time
1 hour

Cooking time
30 minutes

Storage
3 days in the refrigerator

Equipment
Skimmer
Fine-mesh sieve
Meat grinder + large plate
Large blood sausage funnel with a 1¼-in. (3-cm) opening at the base
Instant-read thermometer

Ingredients
1½ lb. (750 g) pork neck (*gorge de porc*)
1¾ oz. (50 g) carrot, thinly sliced
3½ oz. (100 g) onion, thinly sliced
1¾ oz. (50 g) leek (white parts only), thinly sliced
⅔ oz. (18 g) garlic, finely chopped and divided
1½ oz. (40 g) flat-leaf parsley, divided
1 whole clove
4 cups (1 liter) basic broth (see technique p. 74)
4 cups (1 liter) water
5¼ oz. (150 g) cooked chestnuts
6½ ft. (2 m) natural hog casing, 34/36 mm, cleaned (see technique p. 52)
1 lb. 2 oz. (500 g) fresh pig's blood
1 tsp (5 ml) sherry vinegar
3 tsp (15 g) salt
Scant 2 tsp (4.5 g) ground white pepper
¾ tsp (2 g) quatre-épices spice mix
⅛ tsp (0.5 g) ground nutmeg

1 • Cut the pork neck into 1½-in. (4-cm) pieces. Place in a stewpan with the carrot, onion, leek, ⅓ oz. (10 g) garlic, half the parsley, and the clove. Add the broth and water and bring to a boil, skimming off any foam.

2 • Cover the pan with plastic wrap and cook over low heat for about 4 hours, until the meat is easy to crush between your fingers. Add the chestnuts about 10 minutes before the end of the cooking time.

3 • Strain through the fine-mesh sieve, reserving the cooking liquid. Soak the clean casing in ice water for 15 minutes, then drain and cover with plastic wrap.

4 • Grind all the cooked ingredients through the meat grinder fitted with the large plate into a large bowl.

5 • Strain the blood through the fine-mesh sieve and add to the ground meat. Stir until well blended.

6 • Add the remaining garlic and parsley, and the vinegar, salt, pepper, and spices. Stir to combine.

↪

Blood Sausage (continued)

7 • Slide the casing onto the blood sausage funnel. Leave about 4 in. (10 cm) at the end and tie a knot. Hold the casing in place with one hand and block it off at the hole.

8 • Using the other hand, ladle the farce into the funnel.

9 • Gently fill the casing with all the farce, letting it flow in slowly between your fingers. Tie a knot at the end.

10 • Shape into sausages 5–5½ in. (12–14 cm) in length, by pinching and twisting (see technique p. 110); take care not to make them too tight. Bring the reserved broth to a boil in a saucepan. Add the string of sausages and cook, covered, at 185°F (85°C) for 30 minutes. Remove and let cool on a rack. Serve immediately or store in the refrigerator.

Mango Chutney

Makes 1 × 10½-oz. (300-g) jar

Cooking time

About 45 minutes

Storage

3 months at room temperature and 1 year in a sterilized jar

Equipment

Chef's knife

Sterilized 10½-oz. (300-g) jar (see Chefs' Notes p. 105)

Ingredients

Scant 1 cup (225 ml) white vinegar

4 oz. (110 g) onion

¼ oz. (8 g) fresh ginger

1 small clove garlic (2.5 g)

8 oz. (225 g) mango flesh

Scant ½ cup (2¾ oz./75 g) turbinado sugar

⅔ cup (150 ml) veal, chicken, or vegetable stock

Scant 2 tbsp (15 g) raisins

½ tsp (2 g) pectin NH

1 • Bring the vinegar to a boil in a large saucepan and boil until reduced by one-quarter.

CHEFS' NOTES

Served as a condiment, sweet-and-sour chutneys make excellent accompaniments to foie gras, terrines, cheeses, meats, and fish.

2 • Peel the onion and ginger and chop into approximately ⅛-in. (3-mm) dice using the chef's knife. Peel the garlic, remove the germ, and crush. Peel the mango and cut it into dice slightly larger than the onions (just over ⅛ in./4 mm).

↪

Mango Chutney (continued)

3 • Add the sugar, onions, and garlic to the vinegar and cook, stirring regularly, until nearly all the vinegar has evaporated.

4 • Pour in the stock and cook until reduced by half.

5 • Add the diced mango, ginger, raisins, and pectin. Stir to combine.

6 • Let simmer, stirring occasionally, until a thick consistency is obtained. Transfer to the jar, screw the lid on tightly, and let cool.

Homemade Mild Mustard

Makes 3 cups (1½ lb./750 g)

Active time
25 minutes

Fermentation time
1 week

Chilling time
72 hours

Storage
2 months in the refrigerator

Equipment
3-cup (750-ml) jar for fermentation
Blender
Jars for storage

Ingredients

- 1⅓ cups (7 oz./200 g) yellow mustard seeds
- ⅓ cup (1¾ oz./50 g) black mustard seeds
- 1 clove garlic, peeled, germ removed, and crushed
- 2½ tsp (10 g) fleur de sel
- ½ tsp (1.5 g) ground turmeric
- 1½ cups (350 ml) water
- Scant ⅔ cup (140 ml) white wine vinegar

1 • Pour the yellow and black mustard seeds into the 3-cup (750-ml) jar.

2 • Add the garlic.

↪

Homemade Mild Mustard (continued)

3 • Add the fleur de sel and turmeric.

4 • Pour in enough water to just cover and stir until well combined. Add the remaining water.

5 • Prop the lid open so that the jar is three-quarters closed—do not close it completely. Place the jar on a flat surface and let ferment for 1 week at room temperature.

6 • At the end of the fermentation time, pour the mixture into the blender with the vinegar and process to the desired consistency. Adjust the seasoning and transfer to jars of your choice. Chill for 72 hours before using.

Pickled Vegetables

Makes 2 jars

Active time
25 minutes

Cooking time
5 minutes

Resting time
1 week

Storage
1 month in the refrigerator

Equipment
Sterilized jars
(see Chefs' Notes)

Ingredients

Vegetables
Radishes
Spring carrots
Purple carrots
Chioggia beet
Zucchini
Cauliflower
Button mushrooms
Sweet chili pepper

Brine
Scant 2½ cups (600 ml) water
1¼ cups (300 ml) white vinegar
Scant ⅔ cup (4¼ oz./120 g) sugar
4 tsp (20 g) salt
1 clove garlic
½ tbsp peppercorns
1 tbsp coriander seeds
1 tbsp mustard seeds
1 bay leaf
1 sprig thyme

1 • Scrub and/or wash the vegetables and peel if necessary. Score a cross in the base of each radish. Cut the spring carrots in half lengthwise, and cut the purple carrots and beet crosswise into 1/16–1/8-in. (2–3-mm) slices.

2 • Cut the zucchini in half crosswise, then quarter each half lengthwise. Cut the cauliflower into small florets and quarter the mushrooms. Halve the chili peppers lengthwise and remove the seeds.

CHEFS' NOTES

To sterilize the jars, immerse them in boiling water for 20 minutes, then let them dry upside down on a clean, dry dish towel.

↪

Pickled Vegetables (continued)

3 • Pack the vegetables into the sterilized jars to within ½ in. (1 cm) of the top.

4 • To prepare the brine, place the water, vinegar, sugar, and salt in a saucepan.

5 • Peel the garlic, then halve it, remove the germs, and crush it. Add to the saucepan with the peppercorns, coriander and mustard seeds, bay leaf, and thyme. Heat until the sugar and salt have dissolved and the brine begins to boil.

6 • Ladle the still boiling brine into the jars. Close the jars and let cool at room temperature. Let sit in the refrigerator for 1 week before serving.

Super

ASSEMBLING AND DECORATING

Filling and Shaping Sausages

Ingredients

Natural casings, cleaned
(see technique p. 52)

Sausage meat
(see technique p. 80)

Equipment

Sausage stuffer

Sausage pricker

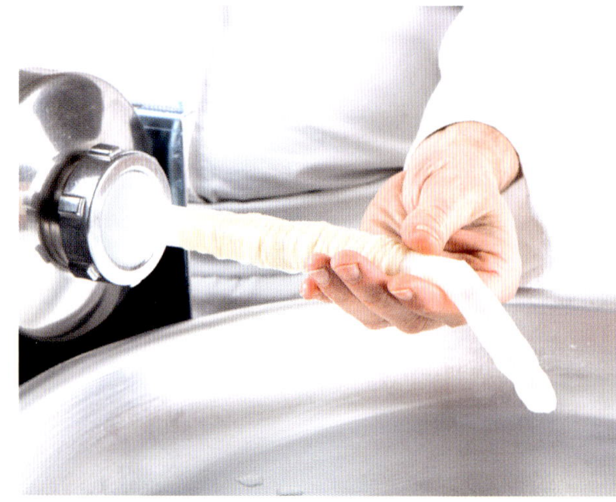

1 • Slide one end of the clean casing onto the filling tube of the sausage stuffer.

2 • Slowly start cranking the stuffer until the meat emerges from the tube into the casing. Tie a knot at the end of the casing, then continue filling it without overstuffing.

3 • When you have used all the sausage meat, cut off the excess casing, leaving 1½–2 in. (4–5 cm) at the end.

4 • Coil the filled casing into a spiral.
Using the sausage pricker, pierce all over to eliminate air bubbles.

5 • Shape into individual sausages by pinching the casing and twisting it two or three times at 4-in. (10-cm) intervals. Take care not to make them too tight.

6 • Repeat until you reach the end of the casing.

7 • Your string of sausages is now ready to cook.

Tying a Roast with Twine

Active time
15 minutes

Equipment
Butcher's twine
Scissors

Ingredients
Top sirloin or topside beef roast (*tende de tranche*), or any other boneless roast

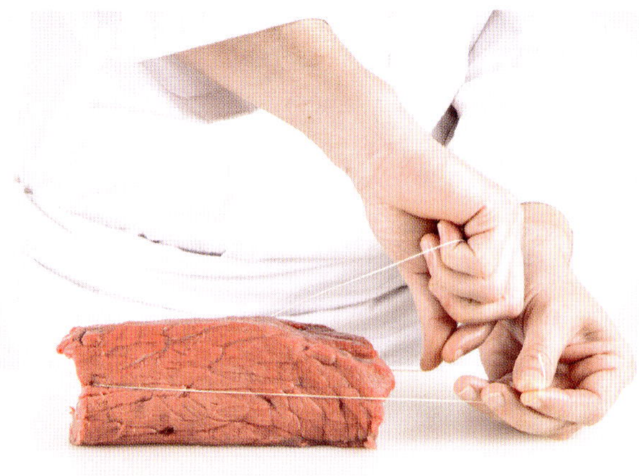

1 • Wrap the twine lengthwise all the way around the meat, about halfway up the sides. Gradually unwind the twine as you go.

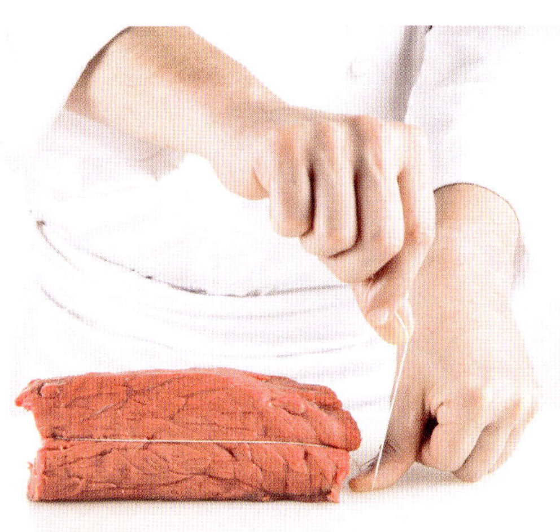

2 • Cross the twine at one end of the meat.

3 • Holding the cut end of the twine in one hand, run the long end underneath the meat.

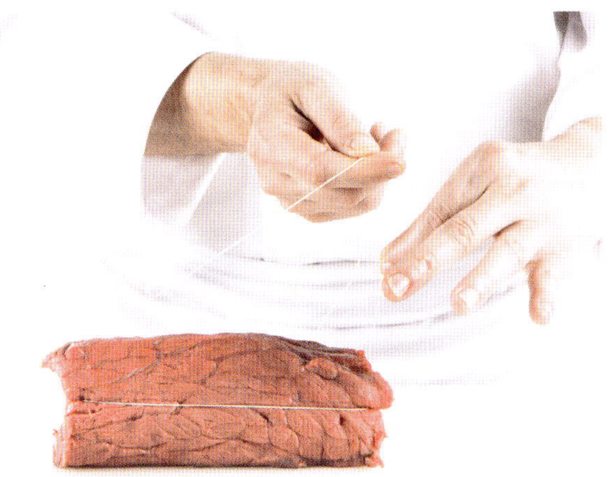

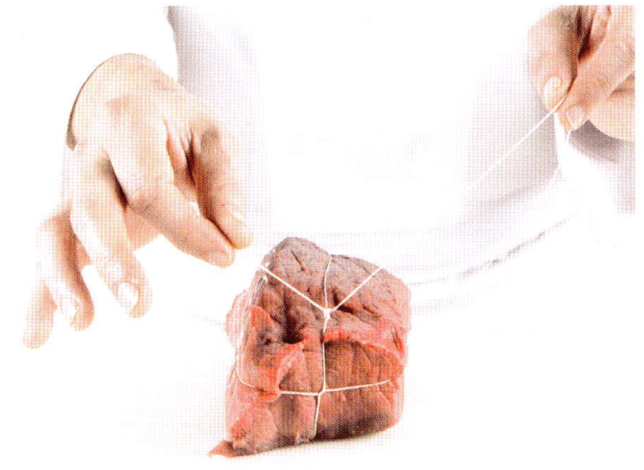

4 • Pull the long end of the twine up and over the meat.

5 • Tie a knot on one side of the top.

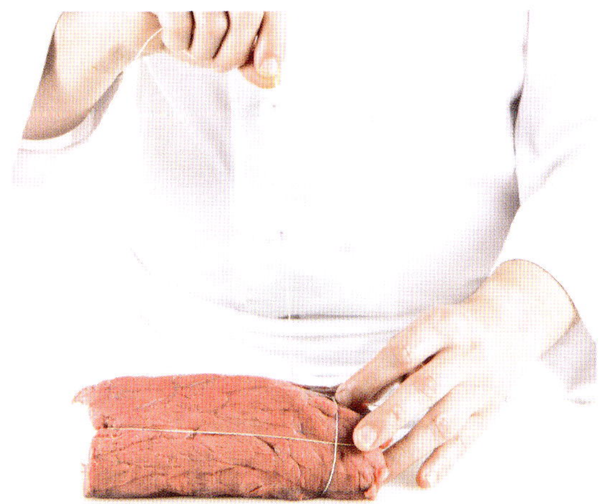

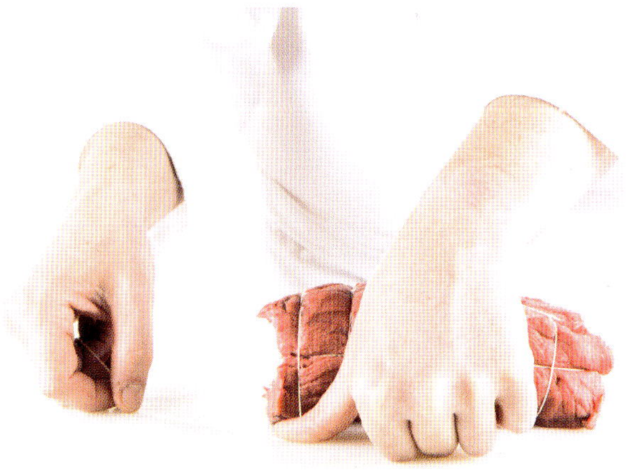

6 • Start wrapping the long end of the twine around the meat.

7 • Continue wrapping the twine around the meat at regular intervals, every ¾ in. (2 cm) or so.

↪

Tying a Roast with Twine (continued)

8 • When you get to the end, return in the opposite direction, wrapping the twine around the meat in between the intervals from the previous step.

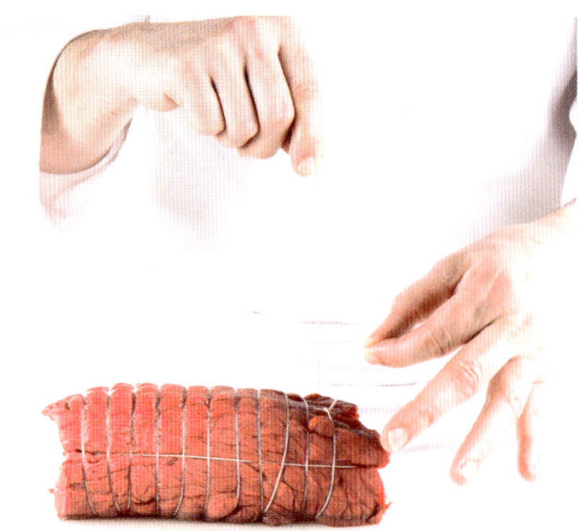

9 • Tie a knot when you reach the end.

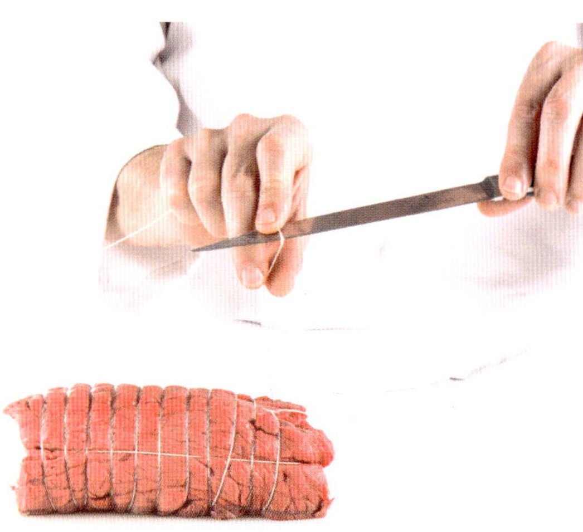

10 • Cut the long end of the twine.

11 • Tie a final knot and trim the excess twine.

Assembling Terrines with Caul Fat

Ingredients

Lard

Farce of your choice

Thinly sliced pork fatback (*barde de porc*)

Fresh herb sprigs of your choice

Caul fat, prepared (see technique p. 54)

Equipment

Terrine mold in the shape of your choice

Disposable glove

Chef's knife

1 • Grease the mold with lard and, wearing the disposable glove, fill it with the farce.

2 • Cut the fatback into 6 strips measuring about ¾ in. (1.5 cm) in width.

3 • Criss-cross the strips of fatback over the farce.

4 • Place the herbs on top and cover with the caul fat.

5 • Trim off the excess caul fat using the chef's knife, leaving some overhanging.

6 • Tuck the overhanging caul fat down between the farce and the inside of the mold. Press down gently on the top to flatten slightly.

Assembling Pâté en Croûte

Ingredients

Pastry for pâté en croûte

Farce of your choice

Egg wash

1 egg

1 egg yolk

2 tsp (10 ml) whole milk

Equipment

Rolling pin

Pâté en croûte mold with hinges

Chef's knife

Ruler

Pastry brush

1 pair disposable gloves

1 • Roll the pastry into a rectangle with a thickness of about ¼ in. (5 mm). Place the mold close to one short side and trim the edge.

2 • Roll the mold over the pastry twice at an angle of 45 degrees, gently pressing down to mark it with the edge of the mold. Cut off the excess pastry, leaving a ¾-in. (2-cm) border on either side. Using the chef's knife, mark the width flush with the mold.

3 • Trim the edges using the ruler as a guide.

4 • Place the pastry in the mold, pressing it against the long sides so it lines them neatly.

5 • Cut two strips from the remaining pastry to line the ends of the mold.

6 • Make the egg wash by whisking together the egg, egg yolk, and milk and brush a little over the edges of the pastry in the mold.

7 • Place the pastry strips at each end of the mold, pressing down on them with your finger to seal the edges well.

↪

Assembling Pâté en Croûte (continued)

8 • Brush the overhanging pastry with egg wash.

9 • Roll the edges inward to form a rim.

10 • Ensure the edges are well sealed.

11 • Fill with the farce of your choice.

12 • Brush egg wash all around the pastry edges, then cut out another rectangle of pastry with the same dimensions as the mold.

13 • Place the pastry on top to make a lid.

14 • Using your finger, press on the dough all around the edges of the farce.

15 • Trim off the excess pastry and brush with egg wash before baking.

Pouring Jellied Broth

Ingredients

Jellied Broth
(see technique p. 70),
warmed until melted

Terrine or pâté en croûte

Equipment

Ladle

Large plain pastry tips

Glass with a pouring spout

1 • **For terrines:** Using a ladle, pour broth over the top until it reaches the edges of the mold or dish.

2 • **For pâté en croûte:** Place the pastry tips in the chimneys and slowly pour in the broth until no more can be absorbed.

Assembling Pies

Ingredients

Quick puff pastry
(see technique p. 58)

Filling of your choice

Egg wash

1 egg

1 egg yolk

2 tsp (10 ml) whole milk

To garnish

Sesame seeds, or other garnish of your choice

Equipment

Rolling pin

2 pan lids, baking rings, or plates with a ¾-in. (2-cm) difference in dia.

Pastry brush

1 • Roll the pastry to a thickness of 1/16 in. (2 mm). Cut out 2 disks.

2 • Place the larger pastry disk on a baking sheet lined with parchment paper. Make the egg wash by whisking together the egg, egg yolk, and milk and brush a border, approximately ¾ in. (2 cm) wide, around the pastry edge.

↪

Assembling Pies (continued)

3 • Place the filling in the center, ensuring it does not cover the egg wash.

4 • Place the second pastry disk on top and fold the edges of the larger pastry disk over it.

5 • Place a piece of parchment paper over the pie and a pizza pan (or similar baking pan) facing down. Carefully flip the pie over.

6 • Brush the pastry with egg wash. Sprinkle with sesame seeds, or the garnish of your choice, then cut a small slit in the top to allow steam to escape.

Decorating Pâté en Croûte

Ingredients

Pâté en croûte

Pastry trimmings

Egg wash

1 egg

1 egg yolk

2 tsp (10 ml) whole milk

Equipment

Pie crimper

Plain pastry tip, about 1/4 in. (5 mm) in dia.

Paring knife

Small plain round cookie cutters of different sizes

Pastry brush

Skewer or pointed tool with a round tip

1 • Make an attractive border using a pie crimper. Crimp the pastry at an angle, at regular intervals all the way around the pâté en croûte.

2 • Using the plain pastry tip, mark the positions for the chimneys, then remove the cut-out pastry using the paring knife.

3 • Cut rings, disks, or other decorative shapes out of the pastry trimmings using the cookie cutters.

4 • Make the egg wash by whisking together the egg, egg yolk, and milk, and brush over the pastry. Place the decorative pastry rings around the chimney holes.

5 • Using the skewer, make small incisions, for example, along the crimped edge of the pastry.

6 • Arrange the decorative pastry shapes over the top of the pastry.

7 • Brush all over with egg wash.

RECIPES

PIES, TARTS, AND PÂTÉS EN CROÛTE

BARBAJUAN-STYLE PITHIVIERS

Pithiviers comme un barbajuan

Serves 6

Active time
1 hour

Chilling time
2 hours

Cooking time
1 hour 10 minutes

Storage
3 days in the refrigerator

Equipment
7-in. (18-cm) baking ring, ¾ in. (2 cm) deep

Ingredients

Green filling

3¼ oz. (90 g) leeks (white parts only)

1¾ oz. (50 g) white onion

Olive oil for cooking + 1 tbsp (15 ml)

9 oz. (250 g) fresh spinach

9 oz. (250 g) Swiss chard greens

3½ tbsp (1¾ oz./50 g) beaten egg (1 egg)

4¾ tsp (4 g) salt

¾ tsp (2 g) ground white pepper

⅛ tsp (0.5 g) ground nutmeg

Scant ¼ cup (1¼ oz./35 g) grated Parmesan

3 oz. (85 g) ricotta

¼ oz. (6 g) chives, snipped

To assemble

1 lb. 5 oz. (600 g) quick puff pastry dough (see technique p. 58)

3½ tbsp (1¾ oz./50 g) lightly beaten egg (1 egg)

1½ tbsp (25 g) egg yolk (about 1 yolk)

2½ tsp (12 ml) heavy cream, min. 35% fat

PREPARING THE GREEN FILLING

Wash and thinly slice the white parts of the leeks. Peel and thinly slice the onion. Sweat both in a Dutch oven with a little olive oil over low heat until softened but not browned, then cover and let cook gently for 20 minutes, until fall-apart tender. Transfer to a bowl, press plastic wrap over the surface, and chill until assembling. De-stem, wash, and drain the spinach and Swiss chard greens and cook in boiling salted water for 3–4 minutes. Drain and refresh in a bowl of ice water. Drain again, pressing to remove as much water as possible, then chop roughly. In a large bowl, combine the onion and leeks with the greens. Add the egg, salt, pepper, nutmeg, Parmesan, ricotta, chives, and 1 tablespoon (15 ml) olive oil. Using a spatula, stir until well blended. Adjust the seasoning if necessary.

ASSEMBLING AND BAKING THE PITHIVIERS

Roll the pastry dough to a thickness of ⅛ in. (3 mm) and cut out one 10-in. (26-cm) disk and one 11-in. (28-cm) disk. Set the smaller disk on a baking sheet lined with parchment paper. Place the baking ring over the center of the disk and fill with the green filling. Whisk together the egg, egg yolk, and cream to make an egg wash and brush over the border of the disk. Remove the ring and lay the larger dough disk over the top. Press down to seal the edges. Using a sharp knife, cut half-moon shapes around the pastry to create a scalloped edge. Brush with egg wash and chill for at least 2 hours. Preheat the oven to 400°F (200°C/Gas Mark 6). Brush the pithiviers again with egg wash and decorate the top as you wish (you can mark curved lines in the pastry with a sharp knife, for example). Bake for 10 minutes, then lower the oven temperature to 350°F (180°C/Gas Mark 4) and continue baking for 20 minutes, before lowering the temperature again to 300°F (150°C/Gas Mark 2) and baking for an additional 15 minutes.

SALMON COULIBIAC WITH BLACK RICE

Koulibiac de saumon, riz vénéré

Serves 6

Active time

1¾ hours

Chilling time

5 hours

Cooking time

2 hours

Storage

3 days
in the refrigerator

Equipment

6-in. (16-cm) skillet

Fine-mesh sieve

Instant-read thermometer

Ingredients

Herb crêpes

1/10 oz. (3 g) flat-leaf parsley

1/10 oz. (3 g) chives

1/10 oz. (3 g) chervil

½ cup (2 oz./60 g) all-purpose flour

¼ tsp (1 g) superfine sugar

¼ tsp (1 g) fine salt

1 pinch (0.25 g) baking soda

3½ tbsp (1¾ oz./50 g) lightly beaten egg (1 egg)

½ cup (125 ml) whole milk

1¾ tsp (8 ml) olive oil

Salmon

1 lb. 2 oz. (500 g) salmon fillet

Salt

Olive oil

Mushroom duxelles

2¾ oz. (75 g) shallots

1/5 oz. (5 g) garlic

1½ lb. (750 g) button mushrooms

2 tbsp (1 oz./30 g) butter

Generous ¾ cup (200 ml) white chicken stock (*fond blanc de volaille*)

Salt and freshly ground pepper

Mushroom sauce

1 oz. (25 g) butter

1 oz. (25 g) all-purpose flour

Generous ½ teaspoon (3 g) fine salt

Scant ½ tsp (1 g) ground white pepper

⅛ tsp (0.5 g) ground nutmeg

Generous 1 cup (250 ml) mushroom duxelles cooking juices (from above)

1 tbsp (15 ml) lemon juice

Wilted spinach

1 lb. 2 oz. (500 g) fresh spinach

2 tbsp (1 oz./30 g) butter

Fine salt

Black rice

1¾ oz. (50 g) shallots

4 tsp (20 ml) olive oil

3½ oz. (100 g) black rice

1 cup (250 ml) white chicken stock (*fond blanc de volaille*)

To assemble

2¼ lb. (1 kg) quick puff pastry (see technique p. 58)

5 hard-boiled eggs

⅔ oz. (20 g) fresh basil leaves

1 egg

1 egg yolk

1 pinch salt

PREPARING THE HERB CRÊPES

Wash and finely chop the herbs. Combine the flour, sugar, salt, and baking soda in a mixing bowl. Whisk in the egg and half the milk until well combined and smooth, then whisk in the remaining milk, oil, and herbs. Chill for 4 hours. Using the 6-in. (16-cm) skillet, make 6 crêpes.

PREPARING THE SALMON

Remove the skin and pin bones from the salmon (see technique p. 45). Trim the fillet into a rectangle measuring approximately 2¾ × 8 in. (7 × 20 cm). Season both sides with salt. Heat a skillet over high heat and briefly sear the salmon on both sides in a little olive oil (ensure the salmon remains raw in the center). Cover with plastic wrap and cool quickly in the refrigerator.

PREPARING THE MUSHROOM DUXELLES

Peel and finely chop the shallots. Peel the garlic, remove the germs, and finely chop. Wash the mushrooms, cut off the bases, and finely chop the tops. Sweat the shallots and garlic in a skillet with the butter, then add the mushrooms and stock and season with salt and pepper. Cover and cook over low heat for 15 minutes. Drain in the fine-mesh sieve, pressing down gently to remove excess liquid. Reserve the cooking juices for the mushroom sauce. Chill the duxelles and juices separately.

PREPARING THE MUSHROOM SAUCE

Melt the butter in a saucepan, stir in the flour, and cook, stirring constantly, without browning. Add the salt, pepper, and nutmeg. Whisking constantly with a small sauce whisk, gradually add a generous 1 cup (250 ml) of the reserved mushroom duxelles cooking juices. Bring to a boil and cook for 2 minutes, stirring constantly. Adjust the seasonings, add the lemon juice, transfer to a container, and press plastic wrap over the surface. Let cool in the refrigerator. Once cooled, stir 1½ oz. (40 g) of the mushroom sauce into the duxelles to bind the mixture together. Reserve ⅔ oz. (20 g) of the mushroom sauce for the spinach and 1½ oz. (40 g) for the rice.

PREPARING THE WILTED SPINACH

De-stem and wash the spinach. Melt the butter in a large saucepan, then stir in the spinach and a little salt. Cover and cook over low heat for 5 minutes. Drain in a colander, pressing down gently to remove excess liquid. Stir ⅔ oz. (20 g) of the reserved mushroom sauce into the spinach to bind it together. Press plastic wrap over the surface and chill until ready to assemble.

PREPARING THE BLACK RICE

Peel and finely chop the shallots. Sweat in a skillet with the olive oil, then add the rice and sauté until translucent. Pour in the stock, cover, and cook over low heat for about 30 minutes, until just cooked. Stir 1½ oz. (40 g) of the reserved mushroom sauce into the rice to bind it together. Press plastic wrap over the surface and chill until ready to assemble.

ASSEMBLING THE COULIBIAC

Peel and chop the hard-boiled egg whites and yolks separately. Combine in a bowl and chill until using. Roll the pastry to a thickness of ⅛ in. (3 mm) and cut out one 9 × 12-in. (22 × 30-cm) rectangle and one 13¾ × 17¾-in. (35 × 45-cm) rectangle. Cover with plastic wrap and chill until using. To prepare the filling, place a large piece of plastic wrap on a work surface and line up 4 crêpes on it, overlapping them slightly. Arrange all the different elements over the crêpes: place a strip of rice the size of the salmon fillet in the center (½ in./1 cm thick). Do the same with the spinach, mushroom duxelles, and chopped eggs, making the layers ¼ in. (5 mm) thick. Place the salmon over the eggs and cover with basil leaves. Top with another layer of chopped egg, followed by a layer of mushroom duxelles, of spinach, and of rice. Wrap up with the 2 remaining crêpes, then cover with the excess plastic wrap, making a log shape. Chill for 2 hours to firm up. Remove the plastic wrap and place the salmon log on the smaller puff pastry rectangle. Whisk the egg, yolk, and salt together to make an egg wash and brush it around the pastry border. Place the second pastry rectangle over the top and press down on the edges to seal, taking care not to make any creases in the pastry. Brush all over with egg wash and cut around the coulibiac to make clean edges. With the pastry trimmings, make a ½-in (1-cm) border to fit around the coulibiac, fix in place with egg wash, and, using a sharp knife, cut half-moon shapes around the band to create a scalloped edge. Brush all over with the egg wash and chill for at least 1 hour. Preheat the oven to 430°F (220°C/Gas Mark 7) and brush again with egg wash. Make a hole in the center to allow steam to escape and score decorative lines in the pastry using the tip of a knife. Bake for 10 minutes, then lower the oven temperature to 350°F (180°C/Gas Mark 4) and continue to bake for 25 minutes, until the pastry is golden brown and the core temperature is 113°F (45°C).

BELLE AURORE PÂTÉ EN CROÛTE

Coussin de la belle Aurore

Serves 12

Active time
45 minutes

Chilling time
24 hours

Cooking time
1 hour 50 minutes

Storage
4 days in the refrigerator

Equipment
Pie crimper
¾-in. (2-cm) plain pastry tip
Instant-read thermometer

Ingredients

Seasoning mix #1
- 2¾ tsp (14 g) fine salt
- 1 tsp (2.5 g) ground white pepper
- ⅛ tsp (0.5 g) ground nutmeg
- Scant ½ tsp (2.5 g) panela (rapadura) sugar

Seasoning mix #2
- 1½ tbsp (24 g) fine salt
- 1¾ tsp (4 g) ground white pepper
- ⅛ tsp (0.5 g) ground nutmeg
- 1 tsp (4 g) panela (rapadura) sugar

Farce
- 14 oz. (400 g) ground pork belly (*poitrine de porc hachée*)
- 2 eggs, divided
- Generous ½ cup (2½ oz./70 g) shelled pistachios, chopped
- ½ cup (120 ml) whole milk, divided
- 14 oz. (400 g) ground veal breast (*poitrine de veau hachée*)
- 9 oz. (250 g) duck breast
- 9 oz. (250 g) guinea fowl breast
- 9 oz. (250 g) foie gras

To assemble
- 10½ oz. (300 g) veal sweetbreads, cleaned (see technique p. 50) and braised
- 3½ oz. (100 g) dried figs
- 4 lb. (1.8 kg) pastry for pâté en croûte (see technique p. 62)
- 2½ oz. (70 g) black truffle bits (*brisures de truffes*, or use finely chopped black trumpet mushrooms)
- 1 egg
- 2 egg yolks
- 14 oz. (400 g) jellied broth (see technique p. 70), warmed

PREPARING SEASONING MIXES #1 AND #2 AND THE FARCE (1 DAY AHEAD)

Combine and weigh the ingredients for seasoning mix #1 and divide equally in two. Combine and weigh the ingredients for seasoning mix # 2 and divide equally into three. Place the pork belly in a bowl, add half of seasoning mix #1, and, using a spatula, stir until well combined. Stir in 1 egg, the pistachios, and half the milk. Press plastic wrap over the surface and chill until assembling. Place the ground veal breast in a clean bowl, add the rest of seasoning mix #1, and stir until well combined. Stir in the second egg and the remaining milk, press plastic wrap over the surface, and chill until assembling. Cut the duck breast into strips about ¾ in. (2 cm) wide (see technique p. 42). Coat with one-third of seasoning mix #2, press plastic wrap over the surface, and chill until assembling. Do the same with the guinea fowl breast. Separate the lobes of the foie gras, devein (see technique p. 48), and season all over with the rest of seasoning mix #2. Press plastic wrap over the surface and chill until assembling.

ASSEMBLING AND BAKING THE PÂTÉ EN CROÛTE

The next day, preheat the oven to 430°F (220°C/Gas Mark 7). Cut the foie gras and sweetbreads into strips about ¾ in. (2 cm) wide. Cut the figs into strips about ¼ in. (5 mm) thick. Divide the pastry into 2 pieces, one about one-quarter bigger than the other. For the base, roll the smaller piece of pastry into an approximately 10 × 14-in. (25 × 35-cm) rectangle, about ¼ in. (6 mm) thick. Roll the larger piece into a rectangle of the same thickness and with approximately 25% longer sides (about 12 × 17 in./31 × 44 cm). If not using the pastry immediately, cover it with plastic wrap and chill until assembling. Place the pastry base (the smaller piece) on a baking sheet lined with parchment paper. Spread all the veal mixture across the pastry, leaving a 1¼-in. (3-cm) border all the way around. Sprinkle with the truffle bits, then arrange the duck, guinea fowl, foie gras, and sweetbread strips over the truffles, alternating them as you go. Top with the pork belly mixture in an even layer. Depending on the size of the pastry base, you can repeat the layers, making sure you finish with a layer of farce. Whisk together the egg and egg yolks for the egg wash and brush around the border. Lay the larger pastry rectangle over the top and gently press around the edges to seal. Trim the sides (by a fraction of an inch/a few millimeters only) to obtain clean edges. Crimp all the way around using the pie crimper, then decorate the top by scoring the pastry with the tip of a knife. Brush all over with egg wash. Using the pastry tip, make a ¾-in. (2-cm) hole in the center to allow steam to escape, then pour in the warmed jellied broth. Place in the oven, lower the temperature to 400°F (200°C/Gas Mark 6), and bake for 35 minutes. Lower the oven temperature again to 195°F (90°C/Gas on lowest setting) and bake for an additional 1¼ hours, until the temperature at the center reaches between 154°F–160°F (68°C–70°C). Chill for 24 hours before serving.

CHICKEN AND VEAL SWEETBREAD PÂTÉ EN CROÛTE

Pâté en croûte volaille et ris de veau

Serves 10

Active time

1 hour

Marinating time

12 hours

Soaking time

1 hour

Cooking time

3 hours

Chilling time

12 hours

Storage

5 days in the refrigerator

Equipment

China cap conical strainer

Disposable gloves

Meat grinder + plate with ¼-in. (6-mm) holes

2¾ × 12-in. (7 × 30-cm) pâté en croûte mold, 3 in. (8 cm) deep

Pie weights

Instant-read thermometer

Ingredients

Marinated meat #1

1½ tsp (8 g) fine salt

½ tsp (2 g) superfine sugar

¼ tsp (1.25 g) ascorbic acid

Scant ½ tsp (1.5 g) ground white pepper

⅛ tsp (0.5 g) five-spice powder

Scant ⅛ tsp (0.25 g) ground nutmeg

10½ oz. (300 g) pork belly (*poitrine de porc*)

7 oz. (200 g) pork neck (*échine de porc*)

2 tbsp (30 ml) white port wine

Marinated meat #2

2 tsp (10 g) fine salt

Scant ¾ tsp (2.5 g) superfine sugar

Scant ½ tsp (1.5 g) ascorbic acid

¾ tsp (2 g) ground white pepper

⅛ tsp (0.5 g) five-spice powder

Scant ⅛ tsp (0.25 g) ground nutmeg

14 oz. (400 g) lower pork shoulder (*épaule de porc*)

9 oz. (250 g) poultry breast of your choice

1½ tbsp (25 ml) white port wine

Farce

Scant ¼ cup (25 g) dried cranberries

1 oz. (25 g) carrot

1 oz. (25 g) white onion

8¾ oz. (250 g) veal sweetbreads

1 tbsp (20 g) butter

3½ tbsp (50 ml) white wine

1½ tbsp (25 ml) white port wine

⅔ cup (150 ml) veal stock

1 bouquet garni

Scant ¼ cup (25 g) shelled, skinned pistachios

⅓ cup (75 ml) reserved sweetbread pan juices

Salt and ground white pepper

Marinated meats #1 and #2 (see above)

3½ tbsp (1¾ oz./50 g) lightly beaten egg (1 egg)

2 tbsp (30 ml) whole milk

To assemble

1 egg

1 egg yolk

2½ tsp (12 ml) heavy cream, min. 35% fat

2½ lb. (1.2 kg) pastry for pâté en croûte (see technique p. 62)

1¼ cups (300 ml) jellied broth (see technique p. 70)

PREPARING THE MARINATED MEAT #1 (1 DAY AHEAD)

Combine the salt, sugar, ascorbic acid, pepper, five spice, and nutmeg in a bowl. Cut the pork belly and upper shoulder into 1¼-in. (3-cm) pieces, place in a bowl, and coat with the seasonings. Add the port wine, press plastic wrap over the surface, and let marinate in the refrigerator for 12 hours.

PREPARING THE MARINATED MEAT #2 (1 DAY AHEAD)

Combine the salt, sugar, ascorbic acid, pepper, five spice, and nutmeg in a bowl. Cut the lower pork shoulder and poultry breast into ¾-in. (2-cm) pieces and coat with the seasoning mix and 1½ tablespoons (25 ml) port wine. Press plastic wrap over the surface and let marinate in the refrigerator for 12 hours.

PREPARING THE FARCE

Soak the cranberries in a bowl of lukewarm water for 1 hour. Drain, cover with plastic wrap, and chill until assembling. Preheat the oven to 400°F (200°C/Gas Mark 6). Peel and finely chop the carrot and onion, saving the trimmings. Prepare the sweetbreads (see technique p. 50) and pierce them in several places using a knife. Sear in an oven-safe skillet or Dutch oven with the butter until lightly browned on all sides, then remove from the pan. In the same pan, sweat the carrots, onions, and trimmings until softened but not browned. Pour off the excess fat and place the sweetbreads over the vegetables. Deglaze with the white wine and reduce, then add the port wine and stock. Add the bouquet garni and season with salt and pepper. Cover and cook in the oven for 20 minutes. Let cool to room temperature, then remove the sweetbreads and strain the pan juices through the conical strainer. Measure out ⅓ cup (75 ml) and set aside. Wearing the disposable gloves, break the sweetbreads apart into pieces, cover with plastic wrap, and chill until assembling. Blanch the pistachios in a saucepan of boiling water for 1 minute, then drain and rinse under cold water. Grind the marinated pork belly and upper shoulder through the meat grinder fitted with the plate with ¼-in. (6-mm) holes. Combine in a large bowl with the marinated pork shoulder and poultry breast, cooked sweetbreads, and egg. Stir in the blanched pistachios, soaked cranberries, milk, and the reserved ⅓ cup (75 ml) sweetbread pan juices. Press plastic wrap over the surface and chill until assembling.

ASSEMBLING AND BAKING THE PÂTÉ EN CROÛTE

Preheat the oven to 275°F (145°C/Gas Mark 1). Whisk together the egg, egg yolk, and cream to make an egg wash. Roll the pastry to a thickness of about ⅛ in. (4 mm) for lining the mold and cut a piece to cover the pâté (see technique p. 118). Line the mold with the dough, brush with egg wash to seal, and place the pie weights in the base. Blind-bake for 40 minutes. Remove and increase the oven temperature to 350°F (180°C/Gas Mark 4). Let the pastry cool, remove the weights, and fill to the top with the pâté. Brush the pastry edges with egg wash and cover with the pastry lid. Seal the edges well, brush the pastry with egg wash, and score an attractive design using the tip of a knife. Make 3 chimneys and decorate with the pastry trimmings (see technique p. 126). Bake for 15 minutes, then lower the oven temperature to 185°F (85°C/Gas on lowest setting) and bake for an additional 1½ hours, or until the temperature at the center reaches 162°F (72°C). Let cool for about 1 hour at room temperature. Meanwhile, warm the jellied broth to 195°F (90°C). While the pâté is still warm, pour the broth slowly into the chimneys until completely absorbed (see technique p. 122). Chill for 12 hours before serving.

BEEF WELLINGTON

Filet de bœuf en croûte

Serves 5

Active time
45 minutes

Cooking time
40 minutes

Cooling time
15–20 minutes

Chilling time
2 hours

Freezing time
15 minutes

Storage
3 days in the refrigerator

Equipment
Lattice dough cutter
Instant-read thermometer

Ingredients

Beef tenderloin
- 1 tbsp (20 g) butter
- 1½ lb. (750 g) center-cut beef tenderloin roast (*rôti de filet de boeuf*)

To assemble
- 1¾ lb. (800 g) quick puff pastry (see technique p. 58)
- 3 oz. (90 g) thinly sliced dry-cured ham
- 7 oz. (200 g) mushroom duxelles (see Salmon Coulibiac recipe, p. 134)
- 1 egg
- 2 egg yolks
- Salt and freshly ground pepper

To serve
- Fresh basil leaves
- Fleur de sel and crushed black pepper

PREPARING THE BEEF

In a skillet with the butter, sear the beef tenderloin until well browned on all sides. Season with salt and pepper. Let cool on a rack for 15–20 minutes, then cover in plastic wrap and chill until assembling.

ASSEMBLING AND BAKING THE BEEF WELLINGTON

Divide the dough into 3 pieces to make one large, one medium-size, and one smaller rectangle. Roll the largest piece into an approximately 14 × 17¾-in. (35 × 45-cm) rectangle, ⅛ in. (3 mm) thick, for the top. Roll the middle piece into an approximately 8 × 12-in. (20 × 30-cm) rectangle, ⅛ in. (3 mm) thick, for the base. Roll the smallest piece into an approximately 6 × 12-in. (15 × 30-cm) rectangle of the same thickness for the decoration. Cover all three with plastic wrap and chill.

Spread a piece of plastic wrap across a work surface and cover with dry-cured ham slices, for rolling up the beef. Spread the mushroom duxelles into a thin, ½-in. (1 cm) layer over the ham. Remove the plastic wrap from the beef and place over the duxelles. Using the plastic wrap, roll the beef up tightly. Close the ends and freeze for 15 minutes to firm up the roll.

Whisk together the egg and egg yolks to make an egg wash. Place the middle-sized pastry rectangle (the base) on a baking sheet lined with parchment paper. Brush around the edges with egg wash, making a 1½-in. (4-cm) border. Remove the plastic wrap from the beef roll and place in the center of the pastry. Cover with the largest pastry rectangle and smooth it over so that it follows the contours of the beef. Gently press around the edges to seal. Trim the edges to obtain a clean rectangle with a maximum border of 1¼ in. (3 cm). Brush all over with egg wash. Roll the lattice dough cutter over the final pastry rectangle, open it out carefully to reveal the lattice pattern, and place over the Wellington. Brush with egg wash and pierce around the border with a wooden toothpick to seal. Chill for 2 hours.

Preheat the oven to 400°F (200°C/Gas Mark 6). Remove the Wellington from the refrigerator and brush again with egg wash. Bake for 10 minutes, then lower the oven temperature to 350°F (180°C/Gas Mark 4) and continue to bake for an additional 30 minutes, until the temperature at the center reaches 113°F (45°C).

TO SERVE

Cut into slices, garnish with basil leaves, and sprinkle the serving plates with fleur de sel and crushed black pepper.

SWEETBREAD, CHICKEN, AND CRAWFISH VOL-AU-VENT

Vol-au-vent

Serves 4

Active time

3 hours

Chilling time

2 hours 50 minutes

Cooking time

3¼ hours

Storage

1 day in the refrigerator

Equipment

Food processor

Fine-mesh sieve

Disposable pastry bag

Steam oven

Instant-read thermometer

Ingredients

Sweetbreads and vegetable filling

14 oz. (400 g) veal sweetbreads

Scant ½ cup (100 ml) white vinegar

7 oz. (200 g) button mushrooms

4 tbsp (2 oz./60 g) butter

5 oz. (150 g) New Zealand spinach

Mousseline farce

9 oz. (250 g) chicken breast meat

Scant ¼ cup (1¾ oz./ 50 g) egg white (about 1⅔ whites)

⅔ cup (150 ml) heavy cream, min. 35% fat, well chilled

⅔ oz. (20 g) truffle, chopped

Salt and freshly ground pepper

Chicken filling

3½ oz. (100 g) chicken kidneys

7 oz. (200 g) rooster comb

Coarse grey sea salt

Scant ½ cup (1¾ oz./50 g) flour

3½ tbsp (50 ml) water

3½ tbsp (50 ml) white vinegar

2 chicken *suprêmes* (airline chicken breasts)

4 chicken wings

Crawfish filling

12 crawfish

3½ oz. (100 g) shallots, chopped

Neutral oil

3½ tbsp (50 ml) cognac

Chicken jus

3½ oz. (100 g) shallots, chopped

5 unpeeled cloves garlic

1 sprig thyme

1 bay leaf

Neutral oil

4 cups (1 liter) water

Vol-au-vent case

1 lb. 2 oz. (500 g) quick puff pastry (see technique p. 58)

1¾ tsp (10 g) egg yolk (about ½ yolk)

3½ tbsp (50 ml) heavy cream, min. 35% fat

To serve

3½ tbsp (50 ml) peanut oil

1 tbsp (20 g) butter

1 large button mushroom, thinly sliced

New Zealand spinach leaves

Marigold petals

PREPARING THE SWEETBREADS AND VEGETABLE FILLING
To blanch the sweetbreads, place in a saucepan of cold water with the vinegar, bring to a boil, and let simmer for 10 minutes. Drain and remove the membranes (see technique p. 50). Place a weight on top and chill for 2 hours. Clean and thinly slice the mushrooms and cook, covered, in a skillet with half the butter and a little water over high heat for 5 minutes. Wash the spinach and wilt it in a separate skillet with the remaining butter.

PREPARING THE MOUSSELINE FARCE
Remove the tendons from the chicken breast, dice it, and process until smooth in the food processor with the egg whites and a little salt. Pass through the fine-mesh sieve into a large bowl. Set over a bed of ice, stir in the cream and truffle, and season with salt and pepper. Place ⅔ oz. (20 g) of the farce in the pastry bag and chill for 30 minutes. Using two small spoons, shape the remaining farce into small quenelles and poach in boiling salted water. Drain on paper towel.

PREPARING THE CHICKEN FILLING
To blanch the kidneys, place in a saucepan of cold salted water, bring to a boil, and let simmer for 10 minutes. Drain and set aside. Rub the rooster comb with coarse salt, rinse well, and place in a saucepan of cold salted water. Bring to a boil and let simmer for 5 minutes. Meanwhile, stir the flour into 3½ tablespoons (50 ml) water in a saucepan until smooth, stir in the vinegar, and season with coarse grey salt. Add the comb, bring to a boil, then let simmer gently in this mixture, covered, over low heat for 1 hour. Meanwhile, preheat the steam oven to 144°F (62°C/Gas on lowest setting). Season the chicken *suprêmes* with salt and pepper and cover with plastic wrap to give them a wing shape. Cook in the steam oven for about 15 minutes, or until the center reaches 144°F (62°C). Cut the chicken wings at the joints into three parts. Remove the two bones from the middle parts (set aside four bones) and fill with the remaining farce. Roll the stuffed wings in plastic wrap, shape into logs, and poach in boiling salted water or steam until cooked. Stick the reserved bones in the stuffed wings to make mini drumsticks.

PREPARING THE CRAWFISH
Devein the crawfish, leaving the shells on. Cook with the shallots and a little oil in a skillet over low heat until the shells turn red, then deglaze with the cognac. Cover and cook for 10 minutes, then remove the crawfish from the pan and peel. Set the meat aside and reserve the shells for the jus.

PREPARING THE CHICKEN JUS
Brown the reserved chicken wing parts and bones in a saucepan with the shallots, garlic, thyme, bay leaf, and a little oil. Add the crawfish shells and water, bring to a boil, and let simmer over low heat for 1 hour. Strain through the fine-mesh sieve into a saucepan and reduce to a demi-glace consistency.

PREPARING THE VOL-AU-VENT CASE
Roll the pastry to a thickness of ¼ in. (5 mm), cut out an 8 × 10-in. (20 × 25-cm) rectangle, and chill for about 20 minutes. Preheat the oven to 350°F (180°C/Gas Mark 4). Whisk together the egg yolk and cream for the egg wash. Make two L-shaped cuts in the pastry rectangle about ½ in. (1 cm) in from the edge along two opposite corners (be sure to leave about ½ in./1 cm at the end of each "L" so as not to obtain a rectangle and a separate border). Bring back each of the "flying" (unattached) corners one over the other, twisting them and pinching the edges to seal. Brush twice with the egg wash, 10 minutes apart. Bake for 20 minutes, until puffed and golden brown, and let cool on a rack.

TO SERVE
In a sauté pan, brown the sweetbreads, chicken *suprêmes* and stuffed wings in the peanut oil and butter. Thinly slice the chicken *suprêmes* at an angle. In a separate skillet, sear the rooster comb and kidneys. Cut the comb into small triangles between the tips of the crest. Cut the center out of the vol-au-vent and attractively arrange all the separate components in the pastry case. Drizzle with chicken jus and decorate with mushroom slices, spinach leaves, and marigold petals.

SAUSAGE IN PUFF PASTRY BRIOCHE WITH RED ONION CONFIT

Saucisson, brioche feuilletée et confit d'oignons

Serves 4

Active time
40 minutes

Chilling time
12 hours

Rising time
2½ hours

Freezing time
30 minutes

Cooking time
1¼ hours

Storage
3 days in the refrigerator

Equipment
Stand mixer + dough hook
2¾ × 8½-in. (7 × 22-cm) loaf pan

Ingredients

Puff pastry brioche dough
1⅔ cups (7 oz./200 g) pastry flour
¼ oz. (8 g) fresh yeast, crumbled
¾ tsp (4 g) salt
2 tbsp (25 g) superfine sugar
¼ cup (2 oz./60 g) lightly beaten egg (about 1 egg), well chilled
¼ cup (60 ml) whole milk, well chilled
3 tbsp (1½ oz./40 g) butter, diced

For laminating
1 stick (4 oz./120 g) butter, preferably 84% fat, diced

Sausage
1 *saucisson Lyonnais*, or another smoked sausage, about 8 in. (20 cm) long and 2 in. (5 cm) thick

Red onion confit
9 oz. (250 g) red onions
2 tsp (10 ml) olive oil
2 tbsp (25 g) panela (rapadura) sugar
1½ tbsp (25 ml) balsamic vinegar
1½ tbsp (25 ml) red wine
Salt and freshly ground pepper

To assemble
Butter for the pan
1 egg
2 egg yolks

PREPARING THE PUFF PASTRY BRIOCHE DOUGH (START 1 DAY AHEAD)

Place all the pastry ingredients except the butter in the bowl of the stand mixer. Knead for 10 minutes on speed 1. Add the 3 tbsp (1½ oz./40 g) butter and knead until just incorporated. Cover the bowl with plastic wrap and let rise for 1 hour at room temperature. Fold the dough over, cover with plastic wrap, and refrigerate for 12 hours. The next day, fold the dough again, then roll it out into a 5 × 11-in. (13 × 28-cm) rectangle and freeze for 30 minutes. Shape the 84% butter into a 5-in (13-cm) square. Place it in the center of the dough and fold the two short ends over it to meet in the center, enclosing the butter completely. Give the dough one double turn, followed by one single turn (see technique p. 58, steps 7–9). Cover in plastic wrap and chill for 30 minutes. Roll the dough into a rectangle that is 2½ in. (6 cm) longer than the sausage on either end and about ⅛ in. (4 mm) thick. Cover with plastic wrap and chill until assembling.

PREPARING THE SAUSAGE

Peel away the casing from the sausage and keep refrigerated until assembling.

PREPARING THE RED ONION CONFIT

Peel and thinly slice the onions and cook in a skillet with the oil over low heat until softened. Add the sugar, cover, and cook over low heat for 20 minutes. Add the vinegar and wine, then cook uncovered for an additional 30 minutes. When the onions are completely tender (they should be easy to crush between your fingers), adjust the seasonings, transfer to a bowl, and press plastic wrap over the surface. Reserve at room temperature until serving.

ASSEMBLING THE SAUSAGE IN BRIOCHE

Grease the loaf pan with butter. Whisk the egg and egg yolks together for the egg wash. Place the sausage in the center of the dough rectangle with a long edge facing you and brush the top edge with egg wash. Roll the sausage up in the dough and trim off excess dough along the seam. Position the seam facing up and roll out the dough ends using a rolling pin to flatten. Brush the ends with egg wash and fold them over to meet in the center of the sausage. Turn over so the seam faces down and place in the loaf pan. Let rise for 1½ hours at warm room temperature (81°F/27°C), away from any drafts, or in an oven. Preheat the oven to 350°F (175°C/Gas Mark 4). Brush the pastry all over with egg wash and bake for 25 minutes, until puffed and golden brown. Serve with the red onion confit and, if you wish, an arugula salad on the side.

PORK, POTATO, AND MOREL MUSHROOM PIE

Tourte de cochon, pommes de terre et morilles

Serves 6

Active time
3 hours

Soaking time
15 minutes

Cooking time
1 hour

Cooling time
1 hour

Chilling time
45 minutes

Storage
4 days in the refrigerator

Equipment
10-in. (25-cm) baking ring, 4 in. (10 cm) deep
Meat grinder + large plate
Steam oven
8-in. (20-cm) baking ring, 4 in. (10 cm) deep
8 × 12-in. (20 × 30-cm) sous vide bag + vacuum sealer machine (optional, see Chefs' Notes)
Box cutter

Ingredients

Pastry
2¼ lb. (1 kg) quick puff pastry dough (see technique p. 58)

Morel mushroom layer
7 oz. (200 g) dried morel mushrooms
1¾ oz. (50 g) shallots
2 tsp (10 g) butter
Scant ½ cup (100 ml) *vin jaune*

Potato layer
1 lb. 2 oz. (500 g) large Charlotte potatoes
Coarse grey sea salt

Pork farce
3 oz. (80 g) shallots
3 cloves garlic
1 bunch flat-leaf parsley
1 lb. 2 oz. (500 g) upper pork shoulder (*échine de porc*)
7 oz. (200 g) fresh pork belly (*poitrine de porc*)
Salt and freshly ground pepper

Egg wash and glaze
2½ tbsp (40 ml) heavy cream, min. 35% fat
1¾ tsp (10 g) egg yolk (about ½ yolk)
Melted butter, to glaze

PREPARING THE PASTRY

Roll the pastry to a thickness of ⅛ in. (3 mm) and cut out 2 disks using the 10-in. (25-cm) baking ring. Chill until assembling.

PREPARING THE MOREL MUSHROOM AND THE POTATO LAYERS

Soak the morels in lukewarm water for 15 minutes. Trim the bases and cut the mushrooms in half lengthwise to be sure they are thoroughly clean. Peel and finely chop the shallots and sweat them in a skillet with the butter over low heat. Add the morels, cover, and cook for 15 minutes. Deglaze with the *vin jaune*. Peel and rinse the potatoes and cut them lengthwise into ¼-in. (5-mm) slices. Blanch in a large saucepan of boiling water with grey sea salt added until they are just tender but still firm.

PREPARING THE PORK FARCE

Peel and finely chop the shallots and garlic. Wash and finely chop the parsley. Cut the pork shoulder and belly into pieces and grind twice through the large plate of the meat grinder into a bowl. Add the shallots, garlic, and parsley and season with salt and pepper. Using your hands, mix until well combined.

ASSEMBLING THE PIE

Preheat the steam oven to 185°F (85°C/Gas at lowest possible setting). Line the base of the 8-in. (20-cm) baking ring with potato slices. Cover with half the farce, followed by half the mushroom mixture. Repeat the layers, finishing with the mushrooms. Slide the ring into the sous vide bag, if using, and vacuum seal. Cook in the steam oven for 50 minutes, then let cool for 1 hour in the bag. Remove the bag and blot off excess moisture using paper towel. Place one of the puff pastry disks on a pie plate or baking sheet lined with parchment paper and set the filled ring on it. Remove the ring and cover with the second puff pastry disk. Using your hands, gently smooth the pastry over the filling to remove air bubbles, dampen the edges with a little water, and press down on them to seal. Use the larger baking ring to cut off the excess pastry and obtain a clean circle. Using the box cutter, cut out equal-sized triangles around the circumference, then make a small cut in the center of each tip. Chill for about 30 minutes.

BAKING THE PIE

Preheat the regular oven to 350°F (180°C/Gas Mark 4). Whisk together the cream and egg yolk to make the egg wash. Remove the pie from the refrigerator and score decorative lines on top from the center to the edge and make a hole in the center. Brush with two layers of egg wash, then chill for another 15 minutes. Brush once more with egg wash and bake for 35 minutes, then lower the oven temperature to 285°F (140°C/Gas Mark 1) and continue to bake for an additional 15 minutes. As soon as you remove the pie from the oven, gently brush it with a little melted butter to glaze.

CHEFS' NOTES

You can steam bake the pie filling without using a sous vide bag and vacuum sealer. This extra step is designed to concentrate the flavors.

DUCK AND MUSHROOM TERRINE

Terrine de canard et champignon

Serves 6

Active time
2 hours

Cooking time
2¼ hours

Storage
1 day in the refrigerator

Equipment
Oval ceramic baking dish, 12 in. (30 cm) long
Fine-mesh sieve

Ingredients

Duck
6½ lb. (3 kg) Muscovy (Barbary) duck, gutted, wishbone removed, and trussed
5 oz. (150 g) carrots
5 oz. (150 g) onions
1 head garlic
Scant ½ cup (100 ml) peanut oil
1 sprig thyme
1 bay leaf
Scant ½ cup (100 ml) white wine
4 cups (1 liter) water
Salt and freshly ground pepper

Additional filling
7 oz. (200 g) dried apricots
14 oz. (400 g) button mushrooms
1 bunch flat-leaf parsley
Olive oil

To assemble
1 lb. 2 oz. (500 g) quick puff pastry dough (see technique p. 58)
1 tbsp (20 g) egg yolk (1 yolk)
2½ tbsp (40 ml) heavy cream, min. 35% fat

PREPARING THE DUCK

Preheat the oven to 350°F (180°C/Gas Mark 4). Season the duck with salt and pepper and roast it in a Dutch oven, covered, for 45–50 minutes, basting occasionally with the drippings. Transfer the duck to a wire rack. Peel and finely chop the carrots and onions and separate the garlic into cloves. Sauté in the Dutch oven with the drippings, peanut oil, thyme, and bay leaf until softened and browned. Remove excess fat and caramelize the brown bits stuck to the bottom of the pan. Deglaze with the white wine, reduce, and add the water. Simmer gently for 25 minutes.

PREPARING THE ADDITIONAL FILLING

Soak the dried apricots in lukewarm water until plump and moist, then drain. Peel, wash, and quarter the mushrooms and wash and finely chop the parsley. Brown the mushrooms in a skillet with a little olive oil over medium-high heat, then stir in the parsley.

ASSEMBLING THE TERRINE

Roll the pastry dough to a thickness of 1/16 in. (2 mm). Cut a strip 2 in. (5 cm) wide and the same length as the circumference of the baking dish, then chill the rest. Whisk together the egg yolk and cream for the egg wash. Brush egg wash over the pastry strip and stick it to the rim of the baking dish—this will help hold the pastry top in place. Separate the legs and breasts from the duck and remove the skin and bones. Cut the leg and thigh meat into large pieces and cut the breasts in three. Roughly chop the duck carcass and return it to the Dutch oven with the pan juices. Simmer for 20 minutes, then strain through the fine-mesh sieve into a saucepan. Reduce to concentrate the flavors, then add the soaked apricots and sautéed mushrooms. Place the duck meat, apricots, and mushrooms in the baking dish and pour in the reduced pan juices. Chill until cold.

BAKING THE TERRINE

Preheat the oven to 340°F (170°C/Gas Mark 3). Cut the remaining rolled-out pastry dough to the size of your baking dish, set it over the terrine, and press the edges together to seal well. Decorate as you wish by scoring a pattern in the pastry and cutting shapes from the pastry scraps. Brush twice with the egg wash and bake for 30 minutes, until the pastry is golden brown. Serve hot.

MIMOSA EGGS ON COMPRESSED CHOUX PASTRY BASES

Œufs mimosa en compression de pâte à choux

Serves 6

Active time

45 minutes

Cooking time

30 minutes

Storage

1 day in the refrigerator

Equipment

2 micro-perforated silicone baking mats

6 × 3-in. (8-cm) baking rings, 3/4 in. (2 cm) deep

Micro-perforated silicone strips

3 disposable pastry bags + 1/3-in. (10-mm) star and plain 1/3-in. (10-mm) tips

Fine-mesh sieve

Ingredients

Choux pastry bases

Scant 1/2 cup (112 ml) water

Scant 1/2 cup (112 ml) whole milk

1 stick (4 oz./115 g) butter, diced

1¼ tsp (6 g) sugar

3/4 tsp (4 g) salt

1 cup plus 1 tbsp (5 oz./140 g) all-purpose flour

1 cup (8 oz./230 g) lightly beaten egg (about 4½ eggs)

Mimosa topping

9 eggs

1 tsp (5 ml) white vinegar

Scant ¼ cup (1¾ oz./50 g) mayonnaise

Salt and ground white pepper

Egg mayonnaise filling

4 eggs

2/3 cup (5¼ oz./150 g) mayonnaise

¼ bunch chives, snipped

Salt and freshly ground pepper

To garnish

2 hard-boiled egg yolks pressed through a fine-mesh sieve

18 × 1/2-in. (1-cm) rounds of cooked egg white

Green clover leaves

Cilantro cress

PREPARING THE CHOUX PASTRY BASES

Preheat the oven to 340°F (170°C/Gas Mark 3) and line a baking sheet with one of the micro-perforated silicone baking mats. Place the baking rings on top and line the sides with micro-perforated silicone strips. Heat the water, milk, butter, sugar, and salt in a saucepan until the butter melts. Bring to a fast boil, remove from the heat, and add all the flour at once. Beat vigorously with a spatula until smooth. Return the saucepan to a low heat and stir constantly for 2 minutes to dry out the mixture. Let cool, then gradually beat in the beaten eggs until smooth and glossy. Spoon into a pastry bag without a tip and pipe 1½ oz. (42 g) of choux pastry dough into each ring. Place the second perforated mat on top, textured side down, and set a weighted baking sheet on top. Bake for 30 minutes, until the choux pastry is golden brown. Remove the rings and pierce a small hole in the center of each pastry base to let steam escape. Let cool on a wire rack.

PREPARING THE MIMOSA TOPPING

Hard-boil the eggs for 10 minutes in a saucepan with water and the vinegar. Drain and plunge into ice water to cool. Peel the eggs and cut them in half lengthwise. Reserve the whites for the egg mayonnaise and press the yolks through the fine-mesh sieve. Combine with the mayonnaise, season with salt and pepper, and transfer to the pastry bag with the 1/3-in. (10-mm) star tip. Chill until ready to assemble.

PREPARING THE EGG MAYONNAISE FILLING

Hard-boil the eggs for 10 minutes in a saucepan, as for the mimosa topping. Drain and plunge into ice water to cool. When the eggs are cold, peel and chop them finely along with the reserved egg whites from the mimosa topping. Stir in the mayonnaise and chives, season with salt and pepper, and transfer to the pastry bag with the 1/3-in. (10-mm) plain tip. Chill until ready to assemble.

ASSEMBLING THE DISH

Pierce holes in each pastry base and pipe in the egg mayonnaise filling. Pipe an attractive swirl of mimosa topping over each one and arrange the garnishes attractively over the top.

CRAB AND AVOCADO CHOUX PUFFS

Choux à l'avocat et au crabe

Makes 10

Active time
45 minutes

Freezing time
10 minutes

Cooking time
30 minutes

Chilling time
30 minutes

Storage
1 day in the refrigerator

Equipment
- 3-in. (8-cm) + 2-in. (5-cm) round cookie cutters
- 2 disposable pastry bags + ½-in. (13-mm) star tip
- Silicone baking mat
- Stand mixer + paddle beater (optional)
- Melon baller
- Food processor

Ingredients

Parmesan craquelin
- 5 tbsp (3 oz./80 g) butter, softened
- Generous ¾ cup (2¾ oz./80 g) finely grated Parmesan
- ⅓ cup (1½ oz./40 g) all-purpose flour

Choux puffs
- ½ cup (125 ml) water
- 4 tbsp (2 oz./60 g) butter, diced
- ½ tsp (2 g) sugar
- Scant ½ tsp (2 g) salt
- ⅓ cup (1½ oz./40 g) all-purpose flour
- Scant ½ cup (3½ oz./110 g) lightly beaten egg (about 2 eggs)

Charcoal shortbread disks
- ¾ cup plus 2 tbsp (3½ oz./100 g) all-purpose flour
- 4 tbsp (2 oz./60 g) butter, diced
- 2 tbsp (30 ml) cold water
- 1 pinch salt
- 1 tsp (2 g) activated charcoal powder (*charbon végétal*)

Crab and avocado puree
- 4 avocados
- Juice and finely grated zest of ½ lime
- Generous ¾ cup (200 ml) heavy cream, min. 35% fat
- 7 oz. (200 g) finely flaked crab meat
- *Piment d'Espelette*
- Salt

To serve
- 1 grapefruit
- 3 red grelot onions
- 3½ oz. (100 g) daikon radish
- 3½ oz. (100 g) flaked crab meat
- 10 avocado marbles
- 10 white garlic flowers
- Cilantro and red-veined sorrel leaves

PREPARING THE PARMESAN CRAQUELIN

Mix the butter, Parmesan, and flour together in a bowl to make a smooth dough. Roll out very thinly between two sheets of parchment paper and freeze for 10 minutes. Cut out 10 disks using the 3-in. (8-cm) round cookie cutter.

PREPARING THE CHOUX PUFFS

Preheat the oven to 340°F (170°C/Gas Mark 3) and line a baking sheet with parchment paper. Heat the water, butter, sugar, and salt in a saucepan until the butter melts. Bring to a fast boil, remove from the heat, and add all the flour at once. Beat vigorously with a spatula until smooth. Return the saucepan to low heat and stir constantly for 2 minutes to dry out the mixture. Let cool, then gradually beat in the eggs until smooth and glossy. Spoon into the pastry bag fitted with the ½-in. (13-mm) star tip and pipe ten 3-in. (8-cm) mounds onto the baking sheet, using up all the pastry. Place a Parmesan disk on each one and bake for 20 minutes, until puffed and golden brown. Let cool completely on a rack before filling.

PREPARING THE CHARCOAL SHORTBREAD DISKS

Preheat the oven to 340°F (170°C/Gas Mark 3) and line a baking sheet with the silicone baking mat. Using the stand mixer, or by hand, beat all the ingredients until they come together into a dough. Roll out thinly between two sheets of parchment paper and chill for 30 minutes. Cut out 10 disks using the 2-in. (5-cm) round cookie cutter, place on the baking sheet, and bake for 15 minutes.

PREPARING THE CRAB AND AVOCADO PUREE

Peel and halve the avocados and remove the pits. Using the melon baller, scoop out 10 avocado "marbles" for garnish. Scoop the remaining flesh into the food processor, add the lime juice, and process to a puree. Transfer to a bowl and stir in the cream using a spatula. Stir in the crab flakes, *piment d'Espelette*, lime zest, and a little salt. Adjust the seasonings as needed and transfer to the second pastry bag fitted with the star tip.

TO SERVE

Peel and segment the grapefruit and thinly slice the onions crosswise. Julienne the daikon radish. Pierce holes in the base of each choux puff and pipe in the crab and avocado puree. Place upside-down (with the hole facing upward) on serving plates and affix the charcoal disks on top with a little of the puree. Garnish each puff attractively with the flaked crab meat, an avocado marble, a grapefruit segment, a red onion slice, and some daikon radish, garlic flowers, cilantro, and red-veined sorrel leaves.

EASTER PÂTÉ WITH SAUCE VERTE

Pâté de pâques, sauce verte

Serves 6

Active time

2 hours

Chilling time

1 hour 40 minutes

Cooking time

About 1 hour

Storage

Up to 3 days in the refrigerator

Equipment

Stand mixer + paddle beater

Meat grinder + large plate

½-in. (1-cm) round cookie cutter

Food processor

Fine-mesh sieve

Ingredients

Pâté crust dough

4 cups (1 lb. 2 oz./500 g) all-purpose flour

1¾ sticks (7 oz./200 g) butter, well chilled and diced

2 tsp (10 g) salt

5 tsp (20 g) sugar

2 egg yolks, at room temperature

⅔ cup (150 ml) hot water

Quail eggs

12 quail eggs

Easter pâté farce

½ onion, finely chopped

Butter

4½ oz. (125 g) veal loin or rump *(quasi de veau)*

9 oz. (250 g) pork belly *(poitrine de porc)*

3½ tbsp (50 ml) cognac

3½ tbsp (50 ml) port wine

¼ bunch flat-leaf parsley

3 sprigs tarragon

1 egg

2 tsp (10 g) salt

2 tsp (5 g) freshly ground pepper

To assemble

4 slices cured ham

2 egg yolks

2 tbsp (30 ml) heavy cream, min. 35% fat

Sauce verte

Parsley stems reserved from the farce

1 bunch chervil

3 sprigs tarragon

1 tsp (4 g) kosher salt

1 egg yolk

1 tsp (5 g) Dijon mustard

⅔ cup (150 ml) peanut oil

⅔ cup (150 ml) olive oil

To serve

Frisée lettuce salad

PREPARING THE PÂTÉ CRUST DOUGH

Place the flour, butter, salt, and sugar in the stand mixer and beat on medium speed until the mixture has the texture of coarse crumbs. Add the egg yolks and hot water, then beat until the dough comes together. Transfer the dough to the work surface, press down on it and push with the heel of your hand, smearing it against the surface until smooth *(fraisage)*. Gather into a ball, cover with plastic wrap, and flatten slightly. Chill for 1 hour before using.

PREPARING THE QUAIL EGGS

Boil the quail eggs for 7 minutes. Place in a bowl of cold water to cool, then remove, peel, and slice off the tips of the eggs to shorten them. Set aside.

PREPARING THE EASTER PÂTÉ FARCE

Sauté the onion in a skillet with a little butter over medium heat until softened and browned. Cut the veal and pork belly into large dice and place in a bowl with the cognac, port wine, and cooked onion. Roughly chop the parsley and tarragon leaves (reserve the parsley stems for the sauce verte) and stir into the bowl. Grind through the large plate of the meat grinder, then stir in the egg, salt, and pepper.

ASSEMBLING AND BAKING THE PÂTÉ

Roll the dough to a thickness of about ¼ in. (5 mm). Cut out two 8 × 12-in. (20 × 30-cm) rectangles, then gather the trimmings together and roll these into a third rectangle of the same size. Chill all three rectangles for 20 minutes.

Using the cookie cutter, cut out equally spaced circles from the third rectangle of dough (see photo), which will be used for decoration. Place one of the remaining rectangles on a baking sheet lined with parchment paper. Spread half of the farce over it, leaving a narrow border. Place the quail eggs end to end in a row down the center of the farce and gently press down on them. Cover with the remaining farce and lay the slices of cured ham over the top. Cover with the remaining rectangle of dough and pinch the edges together to seal well. Prepare an egg wash by whisking the egg yolks and cream together. Brush this over the dough, then carefully pick up the rectangle with holes and place it over the top. Crimp the edges to seal, brush with egg wash, and chill for 20 minutes. Meanwhile, preheat the oven to 400°F (200°C/Gas Mark 6). Brush the dough once more with egg wash and bake for 25 minutes, then lower the oven temperature to 325°F (160°C/Gas Mark 3) and bake for an additional 20 minutes. Transfer to a rack and let cool slightly.

PREPARING THE SAUCE VERTE

Place the parsley stems, chervil, and tarragon in the food processor. Add the salt, egg yolk, and mustard. Pulse until finely chopped. Gradually add the peanut and olive oils and process until smooth and thick. Add a little water to thin the sauce, then strain it through the fine-mesh sieve. Adjust the seasoning and consistency as necessary.

TO SERVE

Cut the pâté into slices and serve warm, accompanied by the sauce verte and a little frisée lettuce salad.

DUCK AND MUSHROOM PIE

Tourte de canard forestière

Serves 6

Active time
40 minutes

Soaking time
20 minutes

Cooking time
40 minutes

Chilling time
2 hours

Storage
3 days in the refrigerator

Equipment
Mandoline
7-in. (18-cm) baking ring, 1¾ in. (4.5 cm) deep
Pie crimper
Large plain pastry tip (optional)

Ingredients

Filling
- 2 confit duck legs
- 5 oz. (150 g) potatoes
- 1¾ oz. (50 g) dried morel mushrooms
- 3 oz. (90 g) fresh morel mushrooms
- 3½ oz. (100 g) shallots
- 3½ tbsp (50 ml) cognac
- 1½ cups (350 ml) heavy cream, min. 35% fat
- 1¾ oz. (50 g) parsley
- ⅓ oz. (10 g) garlic

To assemble
- 1 lb. (450 g) pastry for pâté en croûte (see technique p. 62)
- 6¼ oz. (180 g) quick puff pastry dough (see technique p. 58)
- 1 tbsp plus 2 tsp (25 g) lightly beaten egg (½ egg)
- 1 tbsp (20 g) egg yolk (1 yolk)

PREPARING THE FILLING

Preheat the oven to 400°F (200°C/Gas Mark 6). Remove the excess fat from the duck legs and reserve it. Place the duck legs in a roasting pan and bake for 20 minutes. Remove the skin and bones and shred the meat (see technique p. 44). Peel the potatoes and cut them crosswise into ⅛-in. (3-mm) slices using the mandoline. Blanch for 2 minutes in a large saucepan of boiling salted water, remove the slices with a skimmer, and rinse under cold water to cool. Soak the dried morels in warm water for 20 minutes to rehydrate them, then drain. Wash the fresh morels and cut them and the dried morels in half lengthwise. Peel and finely chop the shallots. Sauté the shallots in a skillet over medium-high heat with a little of the reserved duck fat until softened and browned. Add the fresh and dried morels and deglaze the pan with the cognac. Add the shredded duck, stir in the cream, and cook over low heat for 5 minutes until the liquid has reduced and the mixture is thick and no longer runny. Let cool to room temperature. Roughly chop the parsley. Peel, remove the germs, and chop the garlic. Combine the two in a bowl.

ASSEMBLING AND BAKING THE PIE

Roll the pâté en croute pastry to a thickness of about ¼ in. (5 mm). Set the baking ring on a baking sheet lined with parchment paper and line with the pastry, leaving about ¾ in. (1.5 cm) overhanging. Line the base with half the potato slices and cover with half the duck and mushroom filling. Spread half the garlic and parsley mixture over the duck, then repeat the layers, finishing with the garlic and parsley mixture. Roll out the puff pastry to a thickness of about ¼ in. (5 mm) and cut out a 7¼-in. (18.5-cm) disk. Whisk together the egg and egg yolk to make an egg wash and brush over the edge of the pâté en croûte pastry. Place the puff pastry disk over the pie, pinch the edges of the two pastries together, and brush all over with egg wash. Roll the edges inwards to make a rim and crimp all the way around with the pie crimper. Brush once more with egg wash and chill for 2 hours. Preheat the oven to 400°F (200°C/Gas Mark 6). Using the tip of a sharp knife, score the top of the pastry to make a criss-cross pattern and make a hole in the middle for a chimney to allow steam to escape while baking. Insert a piece of parchment paper rolled into a cylinder or a large plain pastry tip to keep the chimney open (see technique p. 126). Bake for 10 minutes at 400°F (200°C/Gas Mark 6), then lower the oven temperature to 350°F (180°C/Gas Mark 4) and continue to bake for about 30 minutes, until golden brown.

PÂTÉS AND TERRINES

DUCK FOIE GRAS AND FIG MOSAIC

Mosaïque de foie gras de canard aux figues

Serves 10

Active time
50 minutes

Cooking time
35 minutes

Chilling time
72 hours

Storage
12 days in the refrigerator

Equipment
6¼ × 4-in. (16 × 10-cm) terrine mold, 4¼ in. (11 cm) deep
Instant-read thermometer

Ingredients
- 1 lb. 3 oz. (550 g) duck foie gras
- 1½ tsp (7 g) fine salt
- Generous ½ tsp (1.5 g) freshly ground pepper
- ½ tsp (2 g) superfine sugar
- Scant ½ tsp (1 g) paprika
- ⅛ tsp (0.5 g) ground nutmeg
- 5 oz. (150 g) dried figs
- ⅓ cup (80 ml) port wine
- 1 star anise pod
- 1 cinnamon stick
- ¼ tsp (1 g) fleur de sel
- ½ tsp (1 g) coarsely ground pepper
- ⅔ cup (165 ml) water

Using a small knife, remove the two principal veins from the foie gras, taking care to keep the lobes as intact as possible (see technique p. 48).

Sear the foie gras on both sides in a hot, ungreased skillet. Drain on paper towel. Season both sides with the salt, pepper, sugar, paprika, and nutmeg.

Place the figs, port wine, star anise, cinnamon, fleur de sel, and coarsely ground pepper in a saucepan and add the water. Simmer gently for 15 minutes, then drain, transfer to a dish, and let cool to room temperature.

Preheat the oven to 150°F (65°C/Gas on lowest setting). Cut the figs into ¼-in. (5-mm) slices. Arrange the foie gras and figs in the mold in alternating layers, beginning and ending with the foie gras. Press plastic wrap over the surface and pierce holes in it using the tip of a knife. Bake for 20 minutes, until the temperature in the center reaches 131°F (55°C).

Remove from the oven and place a weight on top to compact the mosaic slightly. Chill for at least 72 hours before serving.

MARBLED FOIE GRAS, CHICKEN, AND SQUAB

Marbré de pigeon, volaille et foie gras

Serves 4

Active time

1 hour

Cooking time

3 hours

Chilling time

14 hours

Storage

5 days in the refrigerator

Equipment

Steam oven (or steamer)

1½ × 12-in. (4 × 30-cm) nonstick long pâté en croûte mold, 2½ in. (6 cm) deep

Fine-mesh sieve

Conical sieve lined with muslin

Silicone cube mold (¾ × ¾ in./2 × 2 cm)

Ingredients

Marbled foie gras

2 whole squabs (pigeons)

2 chicken *suprêmes* (airline chicken breasts)

10½ oz. (300 g) foie gras

Salt and freshly ground pepper

Poultry jus

3½ oz. (100 g) shallots

2¼ lb. (1 kg) poultry wings

Generous ¾ cup (200 ml) peanut oil

1 head garlic

1 sprig thyme

1 bay leaf

3 tbsp (1¾ oz./50 g) butter

Squab and chicken jellied cubes

1 onion

1 carrot

1 fresh tomato

1 leek

1 lb. 2 oz. (500 g) chicken carcass

Neutral oil

1 sprig thyme

1 bay leaf

5 juniper berries

3½ tbsp (50 ml) soy sauce

10 sheets gelatin (200 Bloom)

To serve

A few marigold stems with leaves

Fleur de sel and freshly ground pepper

PREPARING THE MARBLED FOIE GRAS

Preheat the steam oven to 160°F (70°C/Gas on lowest setting). Gut the squabs and remove the legs and breast fillets. Reserve the skin, wings, and legs for the jellied cubes. Remove the skin, any bones, and tendons from the chicken *suprêmes*, then remove the tenders. Reserve the skin and tenders for the jellied cubes. Devein the foie gras (see technique p. 48) and shape it into a rectangle that will fit into the mold. Season the foie gras, squab breasts, and chicken *suprêmes* with salt and pepper. Place the *suprêmes* in the base of the mold, cover with the foie gras, and finish with the squab breasts. Press down to compact the meat, then cover with plastic wrap and cook in the steam oven (or steam) for 45 minutes. Let cool completely, then place a weight on top and refrigerate for 12 hours.

PREPARING THE POULTRY JUS

Peel the shallots and cut crosswise into rounds. Roughly chop the wings and brown them in a sauté pan with the peanut oil. Add the shallots, garlic head, thyme, and bay leaf, then stir in the butter. Deglaze with a little water, scraping up the brown bits stuck to the pan. Repeat twice more, then add enough water to cover and let simmer for 40 minutes, skimming regularly. Strain through the fine-mesh sieve into a saucepan and reduce to a demi-glace consistency.

PREPARING THE SQUAB AND CHICKEN JELLIED CUBES

Peel and finely chop the onion and carrot and dice the tomato. Rinse and thinly slice the leek. Roughly chop the reserved legs, wings, and skin of the squabs and the chicken carcass, as well as the skin and tenders of the chicken *suprêmes*. Brown in a sauté pan with a little oil, then add the onion, carrot, tomato, leek, thyme, bay leaf, juniper berries, and soy sauce. Cook at a gentle simmer for 1½ hours. Near the end of the cooking time, soak the gelatin in a bowl of cold water until softened. Strain the broth through the conical sieve lined with muslin into a saucepan and reduce to concentrate the flavors. Squeeze the gelatin to remove excess water and stir it into the hot liquid until dissolved. Pour into the silicone mold and chill for 2 hours until set.

TO SERVE

Arrange two slices of marbled foie gras and two jellied cubes on each serving plate. Add drops of jus in an attractive pattern. Garnish with the marigold stems and sprinkle with fleur de sel and coarsely ground pepper.

GRANDMOTHER-STYLE PÂTÉ

Pâté façon grand-mère

Serves 10

Active time

1½ hours

Resting time

24 hours

Cooking time

4½ hours

Chilling time

36 hours

Storage

20 days in the refrigerator

Equipment

Meat grinder + plates with ½-in. (10-mm) and ⅓-in. (8-mm) holes

Terrine mold in the shape of your choice, with a capacity of approximately 4 cups (1 liter)

Instant-read thermometer

Ingredients

Farce

14 oz. (400 g) poultry liver

14 oz. (400 g) pork neck (*gorge de porc*)

2½ tsp (13 g) fine salt

1 tsp (3 g) ground white pepper

1 packed tsp (4 g) muscovado sugar

Scant ½ tsp (1 g) quatre-épices spice mix

Scant ½ tsp (1 g) ground nutmeg

Scant ½ tsp (1.5 g) ascorbic acid

2½ oz. (70 g) dry sandwich bread

Scant ⅓ cup (70 ml) whole milk

1 oz. (30 g) grey shallots

⅕ oz. (5 g) garlic

2 oz. (60 g) button mushrooms

Goose fat, as needed

2½ tbsp (40 ml) Madeira wine

Leaves of 1 sprig thyme

1½ bay leaves

Scant ⅓ cup (2½ oz./70 g) lightly beaten egg (about 1½ eggs)

Scant ⅓ cup (70 ml) heavy cream, min. 35% fat

½ oz. (15 g) finely chopped flat-leaf parsley

To assemble

Goose fat

Thin slice of pork fatback (*barde de porc*), slightly smaller than the terrine mold

½ cup (2½ oz./70 g) coarsely ground black pepper

1 piece caul fat, rinsed

5 oz. (150 g) jellied broth (see technique p. 70)

PREPARING THE FARCE (START 1 DAY AHEAD)

Remove the veins and connective tissue from the poultry liver. Cut the pork neck into 1½-in. (4-cm) pieces. Combine the salt, pepper, sugar, quatre-épices, and nutmeg in a bowl. Mix the pork neck with half the seasoning mix until well coated. Press plastic wrap over the surface and let rest in the refrigerator for 12–24 hours. Stir the ascorbic acid into the remaining seasoning and toss with the livers until well coated. Press plastic wrap over the surface and let rest in the refrigerator for 24 hours. The next day, cut the bread into 1¼-in. (3-cm) dice and let soak in the milk in a bowl. Peel and finely chop the shallots. Peel the garlic, remove the germs, and finely chop it. Clean and thinly slice the mushrooms. Sweat the shallots in a skillet with a little goose fat, then add the garlic and mushrooms. Cook until the mushrooms release their juices and the liquid evaporates. Let cool to room temperature. Sear the chicken livers in a skillet with a little goose fat over medium-high heat, leaving the centers pink. Deglaze with the Madeira and let cool to room temperature. Grind the pork neck through the meat grinder fitted with the plate with ½-in. (10-mm) holes. Change to the plate with ⅓-in. (8-mm) holes and grind the livers, followed by the shallot and mushroom mixture, thyme, bay leaves, and soaked bread. Combine the two mixtures in a bowl. Using a spatula, or your hands (wearing disposable gloves), mix in the eggs and cream. Stir in the parsley until well blended.

ASSEMBLING THE PÂTÉ

Preheat the oven to 350°F (180°C/Gas Mark 4). Grease the inside of the terrine mold with a thin layer of goose fat and fill with the farce, packing it down well. Top with the pork fatback and sprinkle with the pepper. Cover with the caul fat, tucking it down neatly between the farce and the sides of the mold (see technique p. 116). Bake in a bain-marie for 20 minutes, then lower the oven temperature to 185°F (85°C/Gas on lowest setting) and continue to bake for about 4 hours, until the temperature in the center of the pâté reaches 176°F (80°C). Near the end of the cooking time, warm the jellied broth to 195°F (90°C) in a saucepan. Remove the pâté from the oven, tilt the mold slightly to pour out the excess liquid, and remove any impurities from around the edges. Pour the hot jellied broth over the pâté (see technique p. 122). If you wish, place a plate (or similar) on top to press it down lightly. Chill for 12 hours before serving.

COUNTRY PÂTÉ

Pâté de campagne

Serves 8

Active time

1 hour

Resting time

24 hours

Cooking time

5½ hours

Storage

20 days in the refrigerator

Equipment

Meat grinder + plate with ½-in. (10-mm) holes

Terrine mold in the shape of your choice, with a capacity of approximately 4 cups (1 liter)

Instant-read thermometer

Ingredients

Seasonings

2 tsp (10 g) fine salt

1 tsp (4 g) muscovado sugar

1 tsp (2.5 g) ground white pepper

⅛ tsp (0.5 g) quatre-épices spice mix

⅛ tsp (0.5 g) ground nutmeg

Scant ½ tsp (1.5 g) ascorbic acid

Farce

1¼ lb. (600 g) pork neck (*gorge de porc*), skin removed

5 oz. (150 g) pig's liver

2½ tbsp (40 ml) red wine

⅔ oz. (20 g) shallot

1½ oz. (40 g) onion

⅒ oz. (2 g) garlic

1 tsp (1 g) thyme leaves

2 bay leaves

Lard

½ oz. (15 g) parsley, roughly chopped

⅓ cup (2½ oz./75 g) lightly beaten egg (about 1½ eggs)

2½ tbsp (40 ml) whole milk

To assemble

⅓ oz. (10 g) lard

Thin slice of pork fatback (*barde de porc*)

1 piece caul fat, cleaned (see technique p. 54)

5 oz. (150 g) jellied broth (see technique p. 70)

PREPARING THE SEASONINGS

Combine all the seasonings. Weigh the mixture, then divide into ⅕ oz. (4 g) for the liver and ½ oz. (15 g) for the neck.

PREPARING THE FARCE (START 1 DAY AHEAD)

Cut the neck and liver into 1½-in. (4-cm) pieces. Place in separate bowls and coat with the quantities of seasonings indicated above. Add about 2 tsp (10 ml) of the red wine to the liver and 2 tbsp (30 ml) to the neck. Press plastic wrap over the surface and let rest in the refrigerator for 24 hours. The next day, peel and finely chop the shallot and onion. Peel the garlic, remove the germs, and finely chop it. Sweat all three in a skillet with the thyme, bay leaves, and a little lard. Let cool to room temperature. Grind the liver twice through the meat grinder fitted with the plate with ½-in. (10-mm) holes. Combine the neck, onion and shallot mixture, and parsley, and grind once through the meat grinder with the same plate. Using a spatula, or with your hands (wearing disposable gloves), combine the two mixtures and incorporate the eggs. Gradually add the milk and mix until well combined.

ASSEMBLING AND BAKING THE PÂTÉ

Preheat the oven to 350°F (180°C/Gas Mark 4). Grease the inside of the terrine mold with a thin layer of lard and fill with the farce, packing it down well. Cut the pork fatback into ¾-in. (1.5–2-cm) strips and place them in a criss-cross pattern over the farce. Cover with the caul fat, tucking it down neatly between the farce and the sides of the mold (see technique p. 116). Bake in a bain-marie for 20 minutes, then lower the oven temperature to 185°F (85°C/Gas on lowest setting) and continue to bake for about 5 hours, until the temperature in the center of the pâté reaches 180°F (82°C). Near the end of the cooking time, bring the jellied broth to a simmer in a saucepan. Remove the pâté from the oven, tilt the mold slightly to pour out the excess liquid, and remove any impurities from around the edges. Pour the hot jellied broth over the pâté (see technique p. 122). If you wish, place a plate (or similar) on top to press it down lightly. Chill for 12 hours before serving.

PORK LIVER PÂTÉ

Pâté de foie

Serves 12

Active time
1 hour

Marinating time
24 hours

Infusing time
20 minutes

Cooking time
2¼ hours

Chilling time
2 hours

Storage
10 days in the refrigerator

Equipment
- Meat grinder + plate with ⅛-in. (3-mm) holes
- Instant-read thermometer
- Food processor
- Terrine mold in the shape of your choice, with a capacity of approximately 5 cups (1.2 liters)

Ingredients
- 14 oz. (400 g) pig's liver
- 1½ tbsp (22 g) fine salt
- 1¾ tsp (4 g) ground white pepper
- 1½ packed tsp (6.5 g) muscovado sugar
- ¾ tsp (2 g) smoked paprika
- Scant ½ tsp (1 g) quatre-épices spice mix
- Scant ½ tsp (1 g) ground nutmeg
- Scant ½ tsp (1.5 g) ascorbic acid
- 2½ tbsp (40 ml) Madeira wine
- 1¾ oz. (50 g) onion
- Scant 2½ cups (600 ml) whole milk
- 1 bouquet garni
- 2 lb. (900 g) soft fat from pork belly (*gras de mouille de porc*)
- ⅔ cup (5 oz./150 g) lightly beaten egg (about 3 eggs)
- Lard
- 7 oz. (200 g) jellied broth (optional, see technique p. 70),

PREPARING THE PÂTÉ (START 1 DAY AHEAD)

Remove the veins and connective tissue from the liver and cut into approximately 1½-in. (4-cm) pieces. Season with the salt, pepper, sugar, smoked paprika, quatre-épices, nutmeg, and ascorbic acid. Add the Madeira, press plastic wrap over the surface, and let marinate in the refrigerator for 24 hours. The next day, peel and finely chop the onion. Place in a large saucepan with the milk and bouquet garni and bring to a boil, stirring to prevent the milk from sticking to the pan. Immediately remove from the heat, cover, and let infuse for 20 minutes. Cut the pork belly fat into 1½–2-in. (4–5-cm) pieces and blanch in a saucepan of boiling water for 3 minutes. Drain and grind through the meat grinder fitted with the plate with ⅛-in. (3-mm) holes. Remove the bouquet garni from the milk and let cool or reheat as needed to reach 140°F (60°C). Place the liver and eggs in the food processor and process for 2 minutes. Add the pork belly fat and process for 1 minute. Pour in the milk and onions and process to obtain a smooth mousse-like texture, ensuring the temperature of the mixture does not exceed 113°F (45°C).

ASSEMBLING THE PÂTÉ

Preheat the oven to 325°F (160°C/Gas Mark 3). Grease the inside of the mold with a thin layer of lard and fill with the pâté. Bake in a bain-marie for 15 minutes, then lower the oven temperature to 185°F (85°C/Gas on lowest setting) and continue to bake for about 2 hours, or until the temperature in the center of the pâté reaches 167°F (75°C). Let cool to room temperature, then chill for 2 hours before serving. If you wish, you can glaze the pâté with jellied broth heated to 167°F (75°C), before chilling.

SALMON AND SPINACH TERRINE

Terrine de saumon aux fines herbes

Serves 8

Active time

1 hour

Cooking time

1 hour

Chilling time

12 hours

Storage

5 days in the refrigerator

Equipment

Colander

Blender

2 disposable pastry bags

6-in. (16-cm) square baking frame, 1¾ in. (4.5 cm) deep

Instant-read thermometer

Ingredients

7 oz. (200 g) fresh spinach, divided

2¼ lb. (1 kg) skinless salmon fillet

Salmon mousseline farce

8½ oz. (240 g) salmon trimmings (see above)

Scant 1 cup (240 ml) heavy cream, min. 35% fat, well chilled

1½ tsp (7.5 g) fine salt

Scant ½ tsp (1 g) ground white pepper

1 tbsp plus 2 tsp (25 g) lightly beaten egg (½ egg)

To garnish

Coarsely chopped toasted pistachios

Puffed quinoa

Salt and freshly ground pepper

PREPARING THE SPINACH

Cook half the spinach in a saucepan of boiling salted water for 4–5 minutes. Remove using a skimmer, reserving the water to cook the remaining spinach. Plunge the spinach into a bowl of ice water. Lift out with a skimmer, reserving the ice water, and let drain in the colander, pressing down to remove excess liquid. Finely chop the cooked spinach in the blender, then chill for the green farce. Return the salted water in the saucepan to a boil and add the remaining spinach, poach for a few seconds, then drain immediately and plunge into the ice water. Drain on paper towel and chill until assembling.

PREPARING THE SALMON

Trim the salmon (see technique p. 45) and cut the fillet into two 6-in. (16-cm) squares, with a thickness of ½ in. (1 cm). Reserve the trimmings for the farce. Cover the fillets with plastic wrap and chill until assembling.

PREPARING THE SALMON MOUSSELINE FARCE

Weigh out 8½ oz. (240 g) of the salmon trimmings and use to make the farce with the remaining ingredients (see technique p. 78). Weigh out 11¼ oz. (320 g) of this farce, spoon it into one of the pastry bags, and chill until assembling. Reserve the remaining salmon farce for the green farce.

PREPARING THE GREEN FARCE

Place the remaining salmon farce in the blender with the finely chopped cooked spinach and process until smooth. Spoon into the second pastry bag and chill until assembling.

ASSEMBLING AND BAKING THE TERRINE

Preheat the oven to 175°F (80°C/Gas on lowest setting). Season the salmon rectangles on both sides with salt and pepper. Set the baking frame on a baking sheet and line with heat-resistant plastic wrap to create a "base." Spread a thin layer of salmon farce over the base and cover with a thin layer of green farce. Top with a layer of poached spinach leaves, then add an even layer of salmon fillet. Top the salmon with a layer of spinach leaves, followed by a layer of green farce and the second salmon fillet. Cover with a third layer of spinach leaves and finish with the mousseline farce. Smooth over the top using a spatula and press heat-resistant plastic wrap against the surface. Bake for 45 minutes, until the temperature at the center reaches 149°F (65°C). Let cool in the refrigerator and chill for 12 hours. Before serving, remove the frame and sprinkle with the pistachios and puffed quinoa.

LAYERED VEGETABLE AND OMELET TERRINE

Pressé de légumes aux omelettes

Serves 6

Active time
1½ hours

Cooking time
1½ hours

Chilling time
2 hours

Storage
2 days in the refrigerator

Equipment
8-in. (20-cm) rectangular baking frame, 1½ in. (4 cm) deep
Food processor with a heating element (e.g. Thermomix, optional)
Muslin (optional)

Ingredients

Bell pepper layer
2 red bell peppers
2 yellow bell peppers
Olive oil

Red onion layer
4 red onions
Olive oil
2 tbsp (30 ml) red wine vinegar
2 tbsp (1 oz./30 g) demerara sugar

Spinach layer
14 oz. (400 g) fresh spinach
4 tbsp (2 oz./60 g) butter
2 shallots, finely chopped
Salt and freshly ground pepper

Omelet layers
12 eggs
Salt and freshly ground pepper

Herbed ricotta
3 sheets gelatin
2 cups (1 lb. 2 oz./500 g) ricotta
1 shallot, finely chopped
¼ bunch tarragon, finely chopped
¼ bunch chervil, finely chopped
Salt and freshly ground pepper

Herb-infused oil (optional)
Generous ¾ cup (200 ml) grape-seed oil
3½ oz. (100 g) parsley stems
1 clove garlic

To serve
Red pepper disks
Red onion slices
Mesclun greens

PREPARING THE BELL PEPPER LAYER
Preheat the oven to 350°F (180°C/Gas Mark 4). Coat the peppers with a little olive oil, place on a baking sheet, and roast for about 30 minutes, until the skins can be peeled away easily. Halve and remove the seeds.

PREPARING THE RED ONION LAYER
Peel and finely chop the onions. Cook in a skillet with a little olive oil over medium-low heat until softened and deeply golden. Add the vinegar and sugar, cover, and cook over low heat for about 20 minutes, until very soft. Let cool.

PREPARING THE SPINACH LAYER
Trim and wash the spinach. Wilt the leaves in the butter with the shallots in a saucepan over medium heat. Drain in a colander, pressing down to remove excess liquid. Roughly chop and season with salt and pepper.

PREPARING THE OMELET LAYERS
Beat the eggs, season with salt and pepper, and cook 4 omelets, each slightly larger than the baking frame.

PREPARING THE HERBED RICOTTA
Soak the gelatin in a bowl of cold water until softened. Squeeze to remove excess water, melt over a bain-marie, and stir into the ricotta. Stir in the shallots, tarragon, and chervil. Season with salt and pepper.

PREPARING THE HERB-INFUSED OIL (OPTIONAL)
Place all the ingredients in the bowl of the food processor with a heating element and cook at 160°F (70°C) on speed 2 for 45 minutes. Strain through muslin and chill until 30 minutes before serving.

ASSEMBLING THE TERRINE
Using the baking frame to ensure neat edges, cut the omelets to the same size as the frame. Place the frame on a serving plate and lay the first omelet in it. Cover with a thin layer of herbed ricotta, followed by a layer of roasted bell pepper strips packed tightly together. Add a second omelet and spread with a layer of red onions. Spread a layer of ricotta over a third omelet and place it over the onion layer. Add a layer of spinach, then the remaining ricotta. Top with the fourth omelet. Chill for 2 hours before serving.

TO SERVE
Remove the frame and cut into slices. Garnish each slice with a red pepper disk, red onion slices, and mesclun greens. Serve with herb-infused oil on the side, if desired.

LAYERED VEGETABLE TERRINE

Pressé de légumes

Serves 8

Active time
1 hour

Cooking time
45 minutes

Infusing time
10 minutes

Chilling time
24 hours

Storage
2 days in the refrigerator

Equipment
Butcher's twine
6-in. (15-cm) square baking frame, 1¾ in. (4.5 cm) deep

Ingredients

Vegetables
2 red bell peppers
Olive oil
¾ bunch green asparagus
1 lb. (450 g) fresh peas in the pods
4¼ oz. (120 g) thin French green beans
7 oz. (200 g) baby carrots, tops attached
10 oz. (275 g) broccoli florets
5¼ oz. (150 g) celeriac
3 leeks, white parts only
Salt

Hibiscus jelly
(see Chefs' Notes)
4¼ sheets (8.5 g) gelatin (200 Bloom)
⅔ cup (160 ml) water
⅒ oz. (3 g) dried hibiscus flowers
Fine salt

To serve
Fleur de sel and crushed black pepper

PREPARING THE VEGETABLES

Preheat the oven to 450°F (240°C/Gas Mark 8). Place the bell peppers in a baking dish, drizzle with olive oil, and roast for 10 minutes, rotating regularly for even browning. Immediately cover the peppers in plastic wrap and let cool to room temperature. When they are cool, peel, cut in half, and remove the seeds. Cut the asparagus stalks into lengths the same size as the baking frame. Shell the peas and cook them in salted boiling water (about 2 tsp/10 g salt per 4 cups/liter) for about 5 minutes. Drain, plunge them into ice-cold water to stop the cooking and fix the color. Gently press the peas between your thumb and forefinger to remove the outer skin. Wash the green beans, trim them so they are the same length as the baking frame, and cook in a saucepan of boiling salted water for about 7 minutes, then plunge into ice-cold water. Wash the carrots and broccoli. Peel the celeriac and cut it into ¼-in. (5-mm) slices. Cook all three in boiling salted water until just tender, then drain and plunge into ice-cold water. Roughly chop the broccoli. Wash the leeks, tie them into a bundle using the butcher's twine, and cook in boiling salted water for 10 minutes. Drain, chill in ice-cold water, then cut each one in half lengthwise and trim to the same size as the baking frame.

PREPARING THE HIBISCUS JELLY

Soak the gelatin in a bowl of cold water until softened. Heat the ⅔ cup (160 ml) water and hibiscus flowers in a saucepan. Remove from the heat, cover, and let infuse for 10 minutes. Remove the hibiscus flowers, pressing down on them to recover all the liquid. Squeeze the gelatin to remove excess water and stir it into the hot liquid until dissolved. Season with fine salt.

ASSEMBLING THE TERRINE

Line the baking frame with plastic wrap to make a base and place on a perfectly flat baking sheet. Layer the vegetables inside the frame (asparagus, bell peppers, leeks, green beans, carrots, celeriac, and broccoli), pouring in hibiscus jelly between each layer to just cover the vegetables. Be sure the final layer of vegetables reaches slightly higher than the top of the frame. Cover with a square of parchment paper cut to fit just inside the frame. Place a weight on top to press down gently and chill for 24 hours.

TO SERVE

Remove the frame, cut into slices, and divide between serving plates. Cover each slice with peas. Sprinkle the plates with a little fleur de sel and crushed pepper and add a few drops of hibiscus jelly.

CHEFS' NOTES

You can replace the water and dried hibiscus flowers in the jelly with ⅔ cup (160 ml) clarified vegetable broth or white stock, if desired.

EGGPLANT AND MISO TERRINE

Terrine d'aubergine au miso

Serves 10

Active time
1½ hours

Cooking time
45 minutes

Chilling time
(see Chefs' Notes)
At least 12 hours

Storage
2–3 days in the refrigerator

Equipment
Grill pan
10-in. (25-cm) terrine mold, 4 in. (10 cm) deep

Ingredients

Grilled eggplant
- 5 eggplants
- ⅔ cup (150 ml) olive oil
- Salt

Miso-glazed eggplant
- 2 eggplants
- 3½ oz. (100 g) barley miso
- Salt

Eggplant mousse
- 2 lb. (1 kg) eggplants
- 8 sheets gelatin
- ⅓ cup (80 ml) heavy cream, min. 35% fat
- 2¾ oz. (80 g) barley miso
- 3 scallions, thinly sliced
- Salt and ground white pepper

To serve
- Toasted sesame oil
- 1 tbsp (9 g) golden sesame seeds + extra for the sauce
- Finely grated zest of 1 lime
- 1 small red chili, very finely chopped (optional)

PREPARING THE GRILLED EGGPLANT

Wash the eggplants and cut them lengthwise into ⅛-in. (3-mm) slices. Season with salt and let rest for 10 minutes in the refrigerator. Dip the slices in the olive oil to coat, then sear them on both sides in the grill pan over high heat to mark with scorch lines. Transfer to a wire rack, then drain on paper towel.

PREPARING THE MISO-GLAZED EGGPLANT

Wash the eggplants and cut them lengthwise into ¾-in. (2-cm) slices. Steam for 8 minutes, until tender. Season with salt, then brush both sides with barley miso.

PREPARING THE EGGPLANT MOUSSE

Preheat the oven to 350°F (180°C/Gas Mark 4). Place the eggplants on a baking sheet and roast for 30–45 minutes until tender. When cool enough to handle, cut the eggplants open, scoop out the flesh, and chop roughly. Place 1 lb. 2 oz. (500 g) of the flesh in a bowl (any remaining can be used for another recipe). Soak the gelatin in a bowl of cold water until softened. Heat the cream and barley miso in a saucepan, squeeze the gelatin to remove excess water, and stir in until dissolved. Pour over the eggplant flesh and stir to combine. Stir in the scallions and season with salt and white pepper.

ASSEMBLING THE TERRINE

Line the terrine mold with the grilled eggplant slices, overlapping them slightly and leaving 2 in. (5 cm) overhanging on both sides. Fill the base with a layer of eggplant mousse and cover with a layer of miso-glazed eggplant. Repeat the layers until the mold is full, then fold the overhanging eggplant slices over the top. Cover with plastic wrap and refrigerate for at least 12 hours, or preferably 1–2 days.

TO SERVE

Unmold the terrine and brush the top and sides with sesame oil to make them glossy. Sprinkle with the 1 tablespoon sesame seeds and some of the lime zest. To make the sauce, pour a little sesame oil in a small bowl and add sesame seeds, the remaining lime zest, and chopped chili. Cut the terrine into slices and serve drizzled with the sauce.

CHEFS' NOTES

This terrine is best made 1–2 days before serving.

LAMB TERRINE WITH MINT

Terrine de daube d'agneau à la menthe

Serves 10

Active time

2 hours

Cooking time

2½ hours

Chilling time

12 hours

Storage

5 days in the refrigerator

Equipment

Fine-mesh sieve

Meat grinder + fine plate (optional)

Instant-read thermometer

Conical sieve lined with muslin

Mandoline

10 × 3½-in. (25 × 9-cm) terrine mold, 2¾ in. (7 cm) deep

Blender

Ingredients

Lamb daube

5½ sheets (⅓ oz./11 g) gelatin (200 Bloom)

3½ lb. (1.5 kg) lamb shoulder (*épaule d'agneau*)

5 oz. (150 g) carrots

7 oz. (200 g) white onions

1¾ oz. (50 g) garlic

1 tbsp (15 ml) olive oil

3 cups (750 ml) white wine

Scant 2½ cups (600 ml) white poultry stock (*fond blanc de volaille*)

2 tbsp (1 oz./30 g) egg white (about 1 white)

Salt and freshly ground pepper

Consommé

2 cups (500 ml) clarified lamb cooking juices (reserved from above)

½ oz. (15 g) carrot

½ oz. (15 g) onion

½ oz. (15 g) leek

½ oz. (15 g) celery

1/10 oz. (2.5 g) garlic

2 tbsp (1 oz./30 g) egg white (about 1 white)

To assemble

10½ oz. (300 g) zucchini

Mint vinaigrette

⅕ oz. (4 g) fresh mint

⅔ cup (150 ml) olive oil

3½ tbsp (50 ml) lemon juice

¾ tsp (4 g) fine salt

Scant ½ tsp (1 g) ground white pepper

To serve

A few mint leaves, roughly chopped

Fleur de sel

Coarsely ground pepper

PREPARING THE LAMB DAUBE

Soak the gelatin in cold water until softened. Debone the lamb shoulder, trim off the fat, and cut the meat into 1-in. (2.5-cm) pieces. Peel the carrots and onions and cut them into ¼-in. (5-mm) dice. Peel the garlic, remove the germs, and chop it. Sauté the lamb in a Dutch oven with the olive oil until lightly browned and season with salt and pepper. Remove the meat and set aside at room temperature. Add the carrots, onions, and garlic and sweat until softened but not browned. Deglaze with the white wine and reduce by three-quarters. Return the lamb to the pan and add the stock. Cover and cook over very low heat for about 2 hours, until the meat is completely tender. Remove the meat and let the juices sit briefly to allow the fat to rise to the top. Skim off the fat, then strain the juices through the fine-mesh sieve. Set aside the vegetables for assembling the dish. Reduce the cooking juices to 2 cups (500 ml) and clarify with the egg white. Squeeze the gelatin to remove excess water and stir it into the juices.

PREPARING THE CONSOMMÉ

Peel the carrot, onion, leek, celery, and garlic, as necessary, and chop finely. Place in a bowl and stir in the egg white. Place in a large saucepan and add the cooled lamb cooking juices. Stirring gently, cook until the temperature of the broth reaches about 176°F (80°C). Stop stirring and bring to a simmer: as the egg white coagulates it will rise to the surface and form a "raft." Reduce the heat to low and cook for 10 minutes. Using a ladle, gradually pour the consommé through the conical sieve lined with muslin.

ASSEMBLING THE TERRINE

Wash the zucchini and cut it lengthwise into ⅛-in. (3-mm) slices, using a mandoline. Poach briefly in a large saucepan of boiling salted water, then drain and plunge into a bowl of ice water. Line the mold with the slices, overlapping them slightly. Arrange regular, alternating layers of cooked lamb, vegetables, and consommé in the mold (you won't need to use all the consommé). Cover with zucchini slices and chill for 12 hours before serving.

PREPARING THE MINT VINAIGRETTE

Blend the mint and olive oil together until smooth. In a bowl, combine the lemon juice, salt, and pepper, then gradually whisk in the minted olive oil until emulsified.

TO SERVE

Cut the terrine into ¾-in. (2-cm) slices and place one slice in the center of each plate. Drizzle with mint vinaigrette and sprinkle with mint, fleur de sel, and pepper.

PORK AND PARSLEY TERRINE

Noix persillée

Serves 10

Active time
1½ hours

Brining time
72 hours

Cooking time
6 hours

Chilling time
24 hours

Storage
20 days in the refrigerator

Equipment
Instant-read thermometer
Fine-mesh sieve
Food processor
Half-sphere terrine mold (or pudding basin)

Ingredients

Brined meats
3½ lb. (1.5 kg) pork shoulder (*épaule de porc*)
3½ lb. (1.5 kg) brine (see technique p. 65)
10½ oz. (300 g) fatty pork rind (*couenne grasse de porc*)

Terrine
7 oz. (200 g) grey shallots
⅓ oz. (10 g) garlic
⅔ cup (150 ml) dry white wine
2½ tbsp (40 ml) white wine vinegar
7 oz. (200 g) onions
5¼ oz. (150 g) carrots
5¼ oz. (150 g) leeks
3½ oz. (100 g) celery
1 sprig thyme
2 bay leaves
10½ cups (2.5 liters) basic broth (see technique p. 74)
1 oz. (25 g) flat-leaf parsley
1 oz. (25 g) chervil
Scant 1 tsp (2 g) white peppercorns
Scant ½ tsp (1 g) ground nutmeg

To garnish
Chervil sprigs

BRINING THE MEATS (START 3 DAYS AHEAD)

Using the tip of a knife, pierce the pork shoulder all over and submerge in the brine. Add the rind and let sit for 72 hours in the refrigerator.

PREPARING THE TERRINE

Peel and finely chop the shallots. Peel the garlic, remove the germs, and finely chop. Place the shallots and garlic in a sauté pan with the wine and vinegar and cook over medium-high heat until reduced by three-quarters. Transfer to a bowl, cover with plastic wrap and chill until assembling. Rinse the brined pork shoulder and rind under running water and place in a large saucepan. Peel and cut the onions and carrots into large pieces. Cut the leeks and celery into large pieces as well. Add the vegetables to the pan with the thyme, bay leaves, and broth. Cover with a lid, leaving a slight opening, and cook at 185°F (85°C) for 5 hours, without stirring. Remove the lean meat, fat, and rind separately. Strain the broth through the fine-mesh sieve and measure out 1½ cups (350 ml). Place in a clean saucepan and reduce by about three-quarters (to ⅓ cup/90 ml). Wash and roughly chop the parsley and chervil. Place the fat and rind in the food processor and process briefly, until finely chopped. Incorporate the reduced shallot-wine mixture, peppercorns, and nutmeg, then pour in the reduced broth. Add more salt, if necessary, then stir in the fresh herbs.

ASSEMBLING AND COOKING THE TERRINE

Preheat the oven to 250°F (120°C/Gas Mark ½). Cut the lean meat into pieces weighing approximately 5¼ oz. (150 g) each and arrange in the terrine mold in alternating layers with the fat-shallot-herb mixture. Cover and bake for 1 hour. Let cool in the refrigerator and chill for at least 24 hours. Just before serving, turn the terrine out onto a serving plate and garnish the herb coating that has formed with chervil sprigs.

VEAL SWEETBREAD AND CHICKEN OYSTER LOAF

Biscuit de ris de veau et sot-l'y-laisse

Serves 10

Active time

1½ hours

Cooking time

40 minutes

Storage

3 days in the refrigerator, after cooking

Equipment

Food processor

Fine-mesh sieve

Disposable pastry bag

Steam oven (or steamer)

8-in. (20-cm) square baking frame, 1½ in. (4 cm) deep

Ingredients

Veal sweetbreads

14 oz. (400 g) veal sweetbreads

5 tbsp (2½ oz./75 g) clarified butter

Salt and freshly ground pepper

Chicken oysters

7 oz. (200 g) chicken oysters

5 tbsp (2½ oz./75 g) clarified butter

Salt and freshly ground pepper

Poultry farce

15 oz. (425 g) poultry breast meat of your choice

1 egg white

7 tbsp (3½ oz./100 g) butter, softened

Generous ¾ cup (200 ml) heavy cream, min. 35% fat

1¾ tsp (9 g) salt

1¾ tsp (4 g) freshly ground white pepper

To assemble

4 slices sandwich bread

To serve

7 tbsp (3½ oz./100 g) clarified butter

Shredded white cabbage

Microgreens

PREPARING THE VEAL SWEETBREADS

Place the sweetbreads in a large pan of salted cold water, bring to a boil, and blanch them for 2 minutes. Drain and plunge them into a bowl of ice water to stop them cooking, then peel away the thin membranes. In a skillet over high heat, sauté the sweetbreads in the clarified butter until browned. Season and remove from the pan.

PREPARING THE CHICKEN OYSTERS

In a separate skillet, sauté the chicken oysters in the clarified butter over high heat until browned. Season and remove from the pan, reserving the pan juices for serving.

PREPARING THE POULTRY FARCE

Dice the breast meat, place in the food processor with the egg white, and process until smooth. Incorporate the butter, then pass the mixture through the fine-mesh sieve into a bowl. Place the bowl over a bed of ice and gradually fold in the cream using a spatula. Season with salt and pepper, then transfer to the pastry bag.

ASSEMBLING THE LOAF

Preheat the steam oven to 175°F (80°C/Gas on lowest setting), or use a steamer. Set the baking frame on a baking sheet and line the base completely with slices of sandwich bread. Pipe some farce over the bread to make a ½-in. (1-cm) layer and arrange the sweetbreads and chicken oysters on top. Cover with the remaining farce and finish with another layer of bread. Cover with heat-resistant plastic wrap and steam for 20 minutes.

TO SERVE

Preheat the oven to 300°F (150°C/Gas Mark 2). Remove the plastic wrap and baking frame from the loaf and brown it on both sides in a skillet with the clarified butter. Finish cooking in the oven for 20 minutes. Cut into ½-in. (1-cm) slices and arrange on serving plates with the cabbage and microgreens. Drizzle attractively with the reserved pan juices.

CHEFS' NOTES

You can also make this recipe using individual baking rings.

RABBIT TERRINE WITH DRIED FRUIT CHUTNEY

Terrine de lapin et chutney aux fruits secs

Serves 10

Active time
1½ hours

Cooking time
1 hour

Chilling time
48 hours

Storage
4–5 days in the refrigerator

Equipment
- Meat grinder + medium plate
- Terrine mold in the shape of your choice, with a capacity of approximately 6½ cups (1.5 liters)
- Instant-read thermometer
- Food processor
- Muslin

Ingredients

Farce (makes about 3 lb./1.3 kg)
- ⅔ cup (2¾ oz./80 g) shelled pistachios
- 4 oz. (120 g) dried apricots
- 1 lb. 7 oz. (650 g) rabbit meat
- 9 oz. (250 g) pork neck (*gorge de porc*)
- 9 oz. (250 g) fresh pork belly (*poitrine de porc fraîche*)
- 3½ oz. (100 g) round fillet of veal (*noix de veau*)
- 3½ oz. (100 g) chicken livers
- 3½ oz. (100 g) finely chopped shallots
- Oil
- 1 egg
- Scant ½ cup (100 ml) cognac
- Scant ½ cup (100 ml) white chicken stock (*fond blanc de volaille*)
- 3 tsp (15 g) salt
- Scant 1½ tbsp (10 g) ground black pepper

To assemble
- 5 oz. (150 g) caul fat, rinsed

Fruit chutney
- 1 apple (Red Delicious or similar)
- 6 dried figs
- 6 dried apricots
- 4 limes
- 1¾ oz. (50 g) fresh ginger
- 1¼ cups (300 ml) apple cider vinegar
- ½ cup (3½ oz./100 g) demerara sugar
- 1 bird's eye chili pepper
- 10 whole cloves
- 1 cinnamon stick

To serve
- 10 nasturtium leaves
- 10 baby mustard greens

PREPARING THE FARCE

Preheat the oven to 325°F (160°C/Gas Mark 3). Spread the pistachios across a baking sheet lined with parchment paper and toast them in the oven for 10 minutes. Meanwhile, place the dried apricots in a small saucepan, cover with water, and bring to a boil. Drain and plunge the apricots into a bowl of ice water to stop the cooking. Drain again, cut into 1⁄16-in. (2-mm) dice, and set aside. Cut the rabbit, pork neck, pork belly, and veal into pieces. Devein the chicken livers, remove any connective tissue, and cut into pieces. Fry the shallots in a little oil until softened. Grind all the meats through the meat grinder into a bowl and stir in the egg, cognac, stock, shallots, pistachios, and apricots, without overmixing. Season with the salt and pepper.

ASSEMBLING AND BAKING THE TERRINE

Preheat the oven to 285°F (140°C/Gas Mark 1). Line the terrine mold with caul fat, leaving some overhanging, then fill generously with the farce. Fold the overhanging caul fat over the farce and cover the terrine mold with its lid. Place in a baking dish and add enough hot water to come one-third of the way up the sides of the mold. Bake for about 1 hour, or until the temperature in the center of the terrine reaches 153°F (67°C). Remove the terrine from the bain-marie and let cool to room temperature. Let mature for 48 hours in the refrigerator before serving.

PREPARING THE FRUIT CHUTNEY

Peel and core the apple and cut into ¼-in. (5-mm) dice. Cut the dried figs and apricots into ¼-in. (5-mm) dice, as well. Slice the limes thinly crosswise and peel and roughly chop the ginger. Bring the vinegar to a boil in a saucepan, then add the sugar, lime slices, ginger, chili pepper, cloves and cinnamon stick. Simmer for 2 minutes, stirring until the sugar dissolves. Using a skimmer, transfer the limes, ginger, chili pepper, cloves, and cinnamon stick to the food processor and process until finely chopped. Tie the mixture up tightly in muslin, making a small bag. Immerse in the cooking liquid to infuse. Add the diced apple and dried fruits to the liquid and simmer for 5 minutes. Let cool.

TO SERVE

Cut the terrine into slices and serve with a quenelle of fruit chutney. Garnish with nasturtium and baby mustard leaves.

PORK AND FOIE GRAS NOUGAT WITH WINE GLAZE

Nougat de cochon et foie gras à la lie de vin

Serves 4

Active time
2 hours

Cooking time
3 hours

Chilling time
3 hours

Storage
5 days in the refrigerator

Equipment
Large Dutch oven
Fine-mesh sieve
1¼ × 12-in. (3 × 30-cm) log gutter mold, (2.5 cm) deep
Blender

Ingredients

Nougat
- 2 pigs' ears (*oreilles de cochon*)
- 1 pig's trotter (*pied de cochon*)
- 2 qt. (2 liters) red wine
- ⅔ cup (150 ml) Madeira wine
- 7 oz. (200 g) carrots
- 3 onions
- 3½ oz. (100 g) raw beets
- 6 whole cloves
- 1 cinnamon stick
- 10 peppercorns
- 5 juniper berries
- 1 sprig thyme
- 1 bay leaf
- 1 bouquet garni
- 4 cups (1 liter) water
- 7 oz. (200 g) cooked foie gras
- 2 tbsp (20 g) cornstarch

Red onion jam
- 6 red onions
- 3½ oz. (100 g) black currants
- Scant ½ cup (100 ml) red wine vinegar
- Generous ¾ cup (200 ml) red wine
- 10 coriander seeds
- ¼ cup (1¾ oz./50 g) sugar

To serve
- A few black currants
- Marigold petals
- Marigold leaves
- Black peppercorns

PREPARING THE NOUGAT

Using a razor, shave the hairs off the pigs' ears and rinse well. Blanch the ears by placing them in a large saucepan of cold salted water and bringing to a boil. Let boil for 20 minutes, skimming off any foam that rises to the surface. Combine the red wine and Madeira wine in a saucepan, bring to a boil, and flambé to burn off the alcohol. Peel and cut the carrots, onions, and beets into large dice. Place the pigs' ears and trotter in the Dutch oven and add the vegetables, spices, herbs, bouquet garni, and flambéed wine. Add the water and cook at a gentle simmer for 2 hours, until the meat easily falls off the bones. Lift the meats out of the pan. Remove the thick cartilage from the base of the pigs' ears and cut the rest into pieces. Debone the trotter and cut the meat into small pieces. Place in a bowl and mix with a little of the cooking liquid. Strain the cooking liquid through the fine-mesh sieve into a clean saucepan. Cut the cooked foie gras into ¾-in. (2-cm) dice and gently stir into the bowl. Line the log mold with plastic wrap and fill with the meat mixture. Pour in about ⅔ cup (150 ml) of the still-lukewarm cooking liquid, cover with plastic wrap, and chill for 1 hour. To make the glaze, reduce the remaining cooking liquid and strain it through a fine-mesh sieve. Measure out 2 cups (500 ml) of the liquid and whisk in the cornstarch off the heat. Remove the "nougat" from the log mold, place on a rack, and spoon the glaze over it to coat, reserving any remaining glaze for serving. Chill for 2 hours before serving.

PREPARING THE RED ONION JAM

Peel and finely chop the onions. Place in a large sauté pan with the remaining ingredients and cook until thick and jammy (about 35 minutes). Process to a puree in the blender.

TO SERVE

Place a slice of nougat on each plate alongside a spoonful of red onion jam topped with a few black currants. Garnish with marigold petals and leaves, a few peppercorns, and a drizzle of glaze.

DUCK LIVER FLAN WITH PORT WINE COULIS

Crème de foie de blond de canard et coulis de porto

Serves 10

Active time
1½ hours

Cooking time
25 minutes

Chilling time
4–5 hours

Storage
Up to 3 days in the refrigerator

Equipment
Food processor
Fine-mesh sieve
10 × 3-in. (8-cm) ramekins

Ingredients

Duck liver flan
- 9 oz. (250 g) duck livers (or use chicken livers)
- 2 oz. (60 g) shallots
- 3 tbsp (1¾ oz./50 g) clarified butter
- 4 eggs
- 2 cups (500 ml) heavy cream, min. 35% fat
- 2 tsp (10 g) salt
- 2½ tsp (6 g) ground black pepper

Port wine coulis
- 1⅔ cups (400 ml) port wine
- 1 cup (7 oz./200 g) superfine sugar

To serve
- ½ cup (2¾ oz./80 g) golden raisins (sultanas), soaked in water until plump
- 10 sandwich bread sticks, toasted
- A few pea shoots

PREPARING THE DUCK LIVER FLAN

Preheat the oven to 250°F (130°C/Gas Mark ½). Devein the livers, remove any connective tissue, and roughly chop. Peel and finely chop the shallots. Warm the clarified butter in a skillet over medium-high heat, add the livers, and sear them, leaving the centers pink. Add the shallots and cook briefly, just until softened. Let the mixture cool for a few minutes, then place in the food processor with the eggs, cream, salt, and pepper, and process until smooth. Strain through the fine-mesh sieve into a bowl. Pour a generous ⅓ cup (3 oz./90 g) of the mixture into each ramekin. Cover with heat-resistant plastic wrap and bake in a bain-marie for 25 minutes. Chill for 3–4 hours before serving.

PREPARING THE PORT WINE COULIS

Heat the port wine and sugar in a saucepan until the sugar dissolves and the mixture has reduced to a syrup. Chill for about 1 hour. If the syrup is too thick to pour, add a little water to thin it.

TO SERVE

Pour a little coulis over each flan to cover it. Garnish with the soaked raisins, bread sticks, and pea shoots.

PHEASANT TERRINE

Terrine de faisan

Serves 10

Active time
1 hour

Cooking time
About 2 hours

Chilling time
48 hours

Storage
5–6 days
in the refrigerator

Equipment
Meat grinder + large plate
1½-qt. (1.5-liter) terrine mold with a lid
Instant-read thermometer

Ingredients

Farce
- Scant 1½ cups (7 oz./200 g) whole hazelnuts
- 7 oz. (200 g) horn-of-plenty mushrooms
- Butter
- 2 lb. (900 g) pheasant meat (legs and breast), divided
- 7 oz. (200 g) pork fatback (*barde de porc*)
- 14 oz. (400 g) pork neck (*gorge de porc*)
- 3½ oz. (100 g) chicken livers
- 1¾ oz. (50 g) *lardo di Colonnata* (Italian cured pork fat)
- 1 egg
- 4 tsp (20 ml) cognac
- 4 tsp (20 ml) port wine
- 2 tbsp finely chopped fresh oregano
- 2¾ tsp (14 g) salt per 2¼ lb. (1 kg) farce
- 3½ tsp (8 g) ground black pepper per 2¼ lb. (1 kg) farce

To assemble
- 7 oz. (200 g) thinly sliced smoked bacon

To serve
- Toasted baguette slices

PREPARING THE FARCE

Preheat the oven to 300°F (150°C/Gas Mark 2). Spread the hazelnuts over a baking sheet lined with parchment paper and toast them in the oven for 10 minutes. Clean the mushrooms, sauté them in a skillet with a little butter over medium-high heat until browned, then drain. Weigh out 10½ oz. (300 g) of the pheasant. Cut the pork fatback and pork neck into pieces. Devein the chicken livers, remove any connective tissue, and cut into pieces. Grind the 10½ oz. (300 g) pheasant, pork fatback, pork neck, and livers through the meat grinder into a bowl. Cut the remaining pheasant into small strips (see technique p. 42) and the *lardo* into small, equal-sized dice. Stir the egg, cognac, port wine, mushrooms, hazelnuts, oregano, salt, and pepper into the ground meat, then incorporate the diced *lardo*.

ASSEMBLING AND BAKING THE TERRINE

Preheat the oven to 140°F (60°C/Gas on lowest setting). Line the base of the terrine mold with smoked bacon slices. Cover with a thin layer of farce, then a layer of pheasant strips. Repeat the layers until all the farce and pheasant strips have been used. Completely cover the top of the terrine with bacon slices. Place the lid on the mold and bake for about 1½ hours, until the temperature at the center of the terrine reaches 153°F (67°C). Cool the terrine to room temperature, then let mature for 48 hours in the refrigerator before serving. Serve with toasted baguette slices.

LANGOUSTINE AND WATERCRESS BAVAROIS

Bavarois de cresson et de langoustine

Serves 4

Active time
2 hours

Cooking time
1¾ hours

Chilling time
4 hours

Storage
3 days in the refrigerator

Equipment
Blender
Fine-mesh sieve
Silicone Yule log mold with 2 × 4-in. (5 × 10-cm) cavities
Pestle
Muslin
Instant-read thermometer

Ingredients

Langoustines
4 large langoustines or jumbo shrimp

Watercress bavarois
1 bunch fresh watercress
5 oz. (150 g) potatoes
3½ oz. (100 g) celery
3½ oz. (100 g) onions
2 tbsp (1 oz./30 g) butter
Coarse grey sea salt
7 sheets gelatin (200 Bloom)
2 cups (500 ml) heavy cream, min. 35% fat

Langoustine jelly
1 carrot
2 tomatoes
1 leek
Langoustine claws and shells (from above)
4 tsp (20 ml) olive oil
4 tsp (20 ml) cognac
4 tsp (20 ml) soy sauce
1 generous tbsp (20 g) tomato paste
1 sprig thyme
1 bay leaf
8 peppercorns
4 sheets gelatin (200 Bloom)

To serve
Reserved watercress sprigs

PREPARING THE LANGOUSTINES

Peel the langoustines, reserving the claws and shells for the jelly. Season and wrap each one in plastic wrap, and make log shapes. Steam for 5 minutes, then chill until assembling.

PREPARING THE WATERCRESS BAVAROIS

Wash and sort the watercress, reserving several small sprigs for garnish. Remove the leaves and finely chop the stems. Wash and peel the potatoes and cut into large dice. Thinly slice the celery. Peel and thinly slice the onions. Sweat the onions and celery in a large sauté pan with the butter over low heat. Add the watercress stems and potatoes, and enough water to just cover. Season with coarse grey sea salt and cook for 30 minutes, until the potatoes are tender. Soak the gelatin in a bowl of cold water until softened. Cook the watercress leaves in a saucepan of boiling salted water for 5 minutes, then drain and refresh in a bowl of ice water. Let cool completely, then drain. Transfer the onion and potato mixture to the blender and process until smooth. Add the watercress leaves and pulse to a smooth coulis. Strain through the fine-mesh sieve into a bowl, setting aside a little for serving. Squeeze the gelatin to remove excess water and stir it into the still-warm coulis until dissolved. Whip the cream until it holds firm peaks and fold it into the watercress mixture. Pour into four of the cavities of the Yule log mold and place a cooked langoustine in the center of each. Cover the langoustines with the remaining bavarois mixture and chill for 4 hours.

PREPARING THE LANGOUSTINE JELLY

Peel and finely chop the carrot, finely chop the tomatoes, and thinly slice the leek. Crush the langoustine claws and shells using the pestle, and brown in a saucepan with the olive oil. Add the vegetables and deglaze with the cognac. Pour in enough water to cover, then add the soy sauce, tomato paste, thyme, bay leaf, and peppercorns. Cook at a gentle simmer for 1 hour. Soak the gelatin in a bowl of cold water until softened. Strain the broth through muslin into a bowl. Squeeze the gelatin to remove excess water and, when the broth has cooled to 104°F (40°C), stir in the gelatin until dissolved. Place over a bed of ice to set.

TO SERVE

Brush the watercress leaves with a little olive oil to make them glossy. Unmold the bavarois and place one in the center of each serving plate. Drizzle the reserved watercress coulis backwards and forwards over the top, add a spoonful of langoustine jelly to each plate, and garnish with watercress sprigs.

CELERIAC AND APPLE LOG WITH WALNUT CREAM SAUCE

Bûche de céleri et pommes fruits, crème de noix

Serves 4

Active time

2 hours

Cooking time

1½ hours

Chilling time

4 hours

Storage

3 days in the refrigerator

Equipment

Mandoline

Immersion blender

Blender

3 × 10-in. (8 × 25-cm) Yule log mold, 3 in. (8 cm) deep

Pastry bag + Saint-Honoré tip

Comb

Ingredients

Celeriac log

1 celeriac

5 Golden Delicious apples

Juice of 1 lemon

4 cups (1 liter) low-fat milk

1 pinch grated nutmeg

10 sheets gelatin (200 Bloom)

Generous ¾ cup (200 ml) heavy cream, min. 35% fat, well chilled

Salt and freshly ground pepper

Walnut cream sauce

7 oz. (200 g) walnut halves

Scant ½ cup (100 ml) spring water

3½ tbsp (50 ml) heavy cream, min. 35% fat

Scant ½ cup (100 ml) walnut oil

Salt and freshly ground pepper

To garnish

½ Golden Delicious apple

8 walnut halves

4 sprigs salad burnet

PREPARING THE CELERIAC LOG

Peel the celeriac and cut about 20 thin slices using the mandoline. Blanch briefly in boiling salted water until crisp-tender. Peel and core the apples, coat with lemon juice, and cut slices the same thickness as the celeriac. Cut the remaining celeriac into pieces and place in a saucepan with the milk, nutmeg, and a little water. Cook until completely tender. Meanwhile, soak the gelatin in a bowl of cold water until softened. Drain the celeriac and process to a smooth puree using the immersion blender. Squeeze the gelatin to remove excess water and stir it into the still-warm puree until dissolved. Whip the cream until it holds firm peaks, then whisk it into the celeriac mixture. Season with salt and pepper. Line the inside of the log mold with plastic wrap and arrange a layer of celeriac slices over it. Coat with a layer of celeriac cream and cover with a layer of apples. Repeat the layers until the mold is full. Transfer the remaining celeriac cream to the pastry bag with the Saint Honoré tip and chill until assembling. Cover the log with plastic wrap and chill for 4 hours.

PREPARING THE WALNUT CREAM SAUCE

Toast the walnuts in an ungreased skillet over high heat for 5 minutes. Add the spring water and cook for 10 minutes, then stir in the cream. Pour everything into the blender, process until smooth, and season with salt and pepper. With the blender running, gradually add in the walnut oil and continue blending until emulsified.

PREPARING THE GARNISHES

Preheat the oven to 120°F (50°C/Gas on lowest setting). Using the mandoline, cut the apple into eight 1/16 -in. (2-mm) slices and place on a baking sheet lined with parchment paper. Dry in the oven for 50 minutes. Toast the walnuts in an ungreased skillet over high heat for 5 minutes.

TO SERVE

Remove the log from the mold, cut it into pieces, and place on serving plates. Pipe a swirl of celeriac cream over the top. Spoon a little walnut cream sauce onto the plates and pull lines through it using the comb. Garnish with dried apple slices, walnut pieces, and a sprig of salad burnet.

SALMON AND VEGETABLES IN ASPIC

Aspic de saumon et fines herbes

Serves 2

Active time
20 minutes

Cooking time
3 minutes

Setting time
3 hours + extra time for individual layers

Storage
2 days in the refrigerator

Equipment
2 × 2¾–3-in. (7–8-cm) half-sphere molds
Instant-read thermometer

Ingredients

Soft-boiled eggs
Vinegar
Salt
2 eggs

To assemble
¼ cup (60 ml) clarified jellied broth (see techniques pp. 70 and 76)
1¾ oz. (50 g) cooked peas
2¼ oz. (65 g) smoked salmon slices
1¼ oz. (35 g) cooked broccoli florets
½ oz. (15 g) cooked green beans
½ red bell pepper, peeled and finely chopped

PREPARING THE SOFT-BOILED EGGS

Measure water into a saucepan and add vinegar equal to 3% of the total volume of water. Season with salt and bring to a boil. Carefully lower the eggs into the water using a skimmer and cook them for 3 minutes, until soft-boiled. Remove with the skimmer and drain on paper towel. Chill until assembling.

ASSEMBLING

Melt the clarified jellied broth to a maximum temperature of 95°F (35°C), taking care not to overheat it. Divide the peas between the bases of the half-sphere molds and pour in enough of the clarified broth to just cover them. Let set in the refrigerator. Line the sides of the molds with the smoked salmon. Add broccoli, green beans, and bell pepper in successive layers, pouring in broth to cover for each layer, and letting it set each time in the refrigerator, as for the peas. Peel the eggs and place one in the center of each mold. Finish filling the molds in layers as before, then let set in the refrigerator for at least 3 hours. Just before serving, turn out of the molds onto serving plates and cut in half to display the layers.

BRAWN / HEAD CHEESE

Fromage de tête

Serves 20

Active time
1½ hours

Soaking time
2 hours

Brining time
12 hours

Cooking time
About 7 hours

Infusing time
15–20 minutes

Chilling time
24 hours

Storage
20 days in the refrigerator

Equipment
- Kitchen torch
- Meat injector
- Instant-read thermometer
- Fine-mesh sieve
- Terrine mold in the shape and size of your choice

Ingredients

Brining
- ½ pig's head (*tête de cochon*)
- 12 oz. (350 g) pork cheek (*joue de cochon*)
- 12 oz. (350 g) pork tongue *(langue de cochon)*
- 3 qt. (3 liters) brine (see technique p. 65) at 39°F (4°C)

Cooking
- 9 lb. (4 kg) jellied broth (see technique p. 70)
- 4½ oz. (125 g) onions
- 4½ oz. (125 g) carrots
- 4½ oz. (125 g) celery
- 4½ oz. (125 g) leeks
- 1 head garlic
- Parsley stems
- ⅓ oz. (10 g) fresh thyme
- Bay leaf
- 1 whole clove
- 5 peppercorns

Seasonings
- ¼ oz. (8 g) dried hibiscus flowers
- ⅕ oz. (5 g) chervil
- ⅓ oz. (10 g) parsley
- 1 oz. (25 g) garlic
- 5 oz. (150 g) shallots
- 1 cup (250 ml) dry white wine
- 3 tbsp (45 ml) apple cider vinegar
- ¾ tsp (2 g) ground white pepper
- ⅛ tsp (0.5 g) ground nutmeg
- ⅛ tsp (0.5 g) ground green cardamom
- 1 pinch (0.25 g) ground marjoram

BRINING THE MEAT (1 DAY AHEAD)

Using the kitchen torch, singe off any remaining hairs on the pig's head and scrape clean. Remove the earlobe. Rinse and scrub the head and soak it in cold water for 2 hours. Using the meat injector, inject 1½ cups (360 ml) of the brine into all the meaty parts of the pig's head and the cheek and tongue. Place the head, cheek, and tongue in a container and cover with the remaining brine. Press plastic wrap over the surface and refrigerate for 12 hours.

COOKING THE MEAT

Drain the head, cheek, and tongue, and rinse under cold running water. Place in a large stockpot with the jellied broth. Wash and roughly chop the onions, carrots, celery, and leeks. Add to the pot along with the garlic head cut in half crosswise and the remaining aromatics, and cook at 185°F–195°F (85°C–90°C) for about 6 hours, or until the meat separates easily from the bones but is still slightly firm, and the rind is easy to crush between your fingers. Remove the meat to let the jellied broth cooking juices and fat separate. Cover the meat with plastic wrap and let cool slightly. When cool enough to handle, cut the lean meat (cheek and tongue) into ¾-in. (2-cm) dice, the semi-lean meat (mix of meat and fat) into ½-in. (1-cm) dice, and the fatty parts and rind into ¼-in. (5-mm) dice.

SEASONING THE MEAT

Remove the fat from the jellied broth cooking juices and pour the juices through the fine-mesh sieve. Measure out about 4 cups (1 liter). Add the hibiscus flowers, cover, and let infuse for 15–20 minutes. Wash and roughly chop the chervil and parsley. Peel the garlic, remove the germ, and chop. Peel and finely chop the shallots and cook in the white wine and vinegar until completely reduced, adding the garlic about 5 minutes before the end of the cooking time. Place in a large saucepan with the diced meat and fat from the head and the spices. Warm the hibiscus-infused jellied broth to 176°F (80°C) and add to the pan. Heat everything to a maximum of 195°F (90°C). Remove from the heat, adjust the seasonings, and stir in the chopped fresh herbs.

ASSEMBLING AND BAKING

Preheat the oven to 350°F (180°C/Gas Mark 4). Fill the terrine mold about three-quarters full with the meat, then add hibiscus-infused jellied broth to just cover. Bake for 20 minutes. Let cool to room temperature, then chill for 24 hours before serving.

9.47

RILLETTES AND PULLED MEATS AND FISH

DUCK RILLETTES

Rillettes de canard

Serves 10

Active time
40 minutes

Cooking time
5 hours

Chilling time
8 hours

Storage
20 days in the refrigerator

Equipment
Instant-read thermometer
Fine-mesh sieve
Disposable gloves
Terrine mold in the shape and size of your choice

Ingredients
2 lb. (900 g) duck legs, untrimmed
14 oz. (400 g) skinless, boneless duck breast
4½ oz. (125 g) red onion
2 cloves garlic
4½ oz. (130 g) duck fat
Scant ½ cup (100 ml) water
3½ tbsp (50 ml) duck jus or poultry stock
1 bouquet garni
2 sprigs thyme
2 bay leaves
½ oz. (14 g) Guérande grey sea salt
1 tsp (2.5 g) ground white pepper

Remove the fat and debone the duck legs. Set the bones aside and cut the fat into medium-sized dice. Cut the breast into approximately 1½-in. (4-cm) pieces. Peel and finely chop the onion. Peel the garlic, remove the germs, and chop it.

Melt the diced duck fat with the water in a Dutch oven over medium-high heat. When the water has evaporated, add the meat and brown. Add the 4½ oz. (130 g) duck fat and reduce the heat to low. Add the duck jus or poultry stock, reserved leg bones, onion, garlic, bouquet garni, thyme, and bay leaves. Bring to a boil and sprinkle the salt over the top. Cover with a lid, leaving a slight opening, and cook at 185°F (85°C) for 5 hours, without stirring.

At the end of the cooking time, remove the bones and transfer the meat to a rimmed baking sheet using a skimmer. Strain the pan juices through a fine-mesh sieve into a container with high, straight sides. Let sit for a few minutes to allow the fat to rise to the top, then slowly pour the fat into a small saucepan, stopping before you reach the juices below. Warm the fat over medium heat.

Wearing disposable gloves, shred the duck meat (see technique p. 44) into the terrine mold, then add the pan juices. Gradually pour in the fat (about 20% fat in relation to the meat), stirring continuously with a spatula. Stir in the pepper and adjust the seasonings if necessary. Cover and chill for 8 hours before serving.

PORK RILLETTES WITH PIMENT D'ESPELETTE

Rillettes de porc au piment d'Espelette

Serves 10

Active time
40 minutes

Cooking time
5 hours

Chilling time
8 hours

Storage
20 days in the refrigerator

Equipment
Instant-read thermometer
Disposable gloves
Terrine mold in the shape and size of your choice

Ingredients
- 5 oz. (150 g) white onions
- 1½ cloves garlic
- 13 oz. (375 g) bone-in pork belly (*poitrine de porc*)
- 10½ oz. (300 g) bone-in pork shoulder (*épaule de porc*)
- 8 oz. (225 g) bone-in middle pork shoulder (*palette de porc*)
- 4 oz. (120 g) hard pork fatback (*gras dur de porc*)
- ⅔ cup (160 ml) water, divided
- 10½ oz. (300 g) lard
- 1½ bay leaves
- 1½ sprigs thyme
- 2½ tsp (12 g) Guérande grey sea salt
- 1 tsp (2.5 g) ground white pepper
- 1 tsp (2.5 g) *piment d'Espelette*

Peel and finely chop the onions. Peel and crush the garlic. Remove the skin and bones from the meat (reserve the pork belly bones) and cut the meat into approximately 1½-in. (4-cm) pieces. Cut the fatback into ½-in. (1-cm) pieces. In a heavy-based Dutch oven, melt the fatback with 3 tablespoons (40 ml) of the water over low heat. Add the lard and turn up the heat to medium-high. When the lard has melted, gradually add the meats and cook until lightly browned, stirring often. When the juices are clear, reduce the heat and spread the meat evenly across the base of the pan. Add the onion, garlic, bay leaves, and thyme and sprinkle with the salt. Place the pork belly bones on top and pour in the remaining water. Cover with the lid, leaving a slight opening, and let cook for 5 hours at 185°F (85°C), without stirring.

At the end of the cooking time, remove the bones, lift out the meat with a skimmer, and transfer to a baking sheet. Pour the pan juices into a container with high, straight sides. Let sit until the fat rises to the top, then slowly pour the fat into a small saucepan, stopping before you reach the juices below. Warm the fat over medium heat. Wearing the disposable gloves, shred the meat (see technique p. 44) and return to the Dutch oven. Add the pan juices and gradually pour in the fat, stirring continuously with a spatula. Add the pepper and *piment d'Espelette* and adjust the seasonings if necessary. Transfer to the terrine mold, making sure the fat and meat are evenly distributed. Chill for 8 hours before serving.

MACKEREL RILLETTES WITH LIME

Rillettes de maquereaux citronné

Serves 4

Active time
25 minutes

Cooking time
10 minutes

Storage
3 days in the refrigerator

Equipment
Boning knife
Microplane grater

Ingredients
1 lb. 2 oz. (500 g) mackerel
2 tsp (10 ml) white vinegar
Olive oil
½ bunch chives
¼ bunch dill
1 lime
Scant ½ cup (3½ oz./100 g) mascarpone
Salt and freshly ground pepper
Toasted baguette slices

Using the boning knife, fillet the mackerel and remove any pin bones (see technique p. 45).

Soak the fillets skin side down in the vinegar for 10 minutes, then gently remove the skin.

Fry the fillets in a skillet with a little olive oil over medium heat until the flesh is just cooked through but soft. Place in a bowl and mash with a fork until broken up.

Snip the chives into small pieces, finely chop the dill, and finely grate the zest of the lime. Add all three to the mackerel and stir to combine.

Stir in the mascarpone to loosen, then drizzle with a little olive oil and season with salt and pepper. Stir to blend.

Serve in an empty sardine tin, if you wish, with toasted baguette slices on the side.

VEGETARIAN CARROT RILLETTES

Rillettes végétales de carotte

Serves 6

Active time

45 minutes

Chilling time

24 hours

Storage

3 days in the refrigerator

Equipment

Grater with large holes

Microplane grater

Ingredients

Carrot rillettes

14 oz. (400 g) carrots

1 shallot

1/2-in. (1-cm) piece fresh ginger, peeled

Generous 3/4 cup (200 ml) carrot juice

1/2 cup (3 1/2 oz./100 g) peanut butter or tahini

Juice of 1 lime

Scant 1/2 cup (3 1/2 oz./100 g) ricotta

1/2 cup (1 1/2 oz./40 g) rolled oats

2 tbsp chopped fresh cilantro

10 mint leaves, finely chopped

Piment d'Espelette

Salt

To serve

Microgreens

Toasted bread or multi-seed crackers

PREPARING THE CARROT RILLETTES

Peel and rinse the carrots, then grate them using the grater with large holes. Peel and finely chop the shallot and grate the ginger using the Microplane (you should have about 1/2 teaspoon). Place the grated carrots, shallot, and ginger in a saucepan and add the carrot juice. Cook over low heat until the vegetables are tender, then remove and let cool. In a bowl, combine the peanut butter or tahini with the lime juice, ricotta, and oats. Add the cooled carrot mixture, cilantro, and mint and season with *piment d'Espelette* and salt. Stir lightly until well combined. Taste and adjust the seasonings if necessary. Cover and chill for 24 hours before serving.

TO SERVE

Garnish with microgreens and serve with toasted bread slices or multi-seed crackers.

RABBIT RILLETTES

Rillettes de lapin

Serves 10

Active time
2 hours

Cooking time
1½ hours

Chilling time
24–36 hours

Storage
8 days
in the refrigerator

Equipment
Fine-mesh sieve

Terrine mold in the size and capacity of your choice, or small cast-iron Dutch oven

Ingredients

Rabbit rillettes
1 carrot

1 onion

5¼ oz. (150 g) smoked bacon

Scant ⅓ cup (70 ml) olive oil

9-lb. (4-kg) rabbit, preferably Rex du Poitou, skinned and cut into 8 pieces

3 tbsp (1¾ oz./50 g) wholegrain mustard

1½ cups (350 ml) Sauvignon Blanc

About 4 cups (1 liter) white chicken stock (*fond blanc de volaille*)

½ calf's foot

2 sprigs thyme

1 bay leaf

2 tbsp finely chopped parsley

2 tbsp finely chopped chervil

1 tbsp finely chopped tarragon

Salt and freshly ground pepper

To serve
10 slices toasted country bread

2 oz. (50 g) lightly dressed mesclun greens

PREPARING THE RABBIT RILLETTES

Preheat the oven to 340°F (170°C/Gas Mark 3). Peel and quarter the carrot. Peel and finely chop the onion. Cut the bacon into *lardons*. Warm the olive oil in a Dutch oven over high heat and, when hot, brown the rabbit pieces all over. Add the carrot, onion, and *lardons*, reduce the heat, and cook until the vegetables are softened. Add the mustard and cook until lightly browned. Deglaze with the wine and reduce by a third. Add enough chicken stock to just cover the meats and vegetables and bring to a boil. Add the calf's foot, thyme, and bay leaf. Cover and cook in the oven for 1½ hours. Carefully transfer the rabbit pieces to a plate and discard the aromatics and calf's foot. Strain the pan juices through the fine-mesh sieve into a bowl and skim the fat off the surface (see Chefs' Notes). Taste, reduce the juices further if necessary, and season with salt and pepper as needed. Remove the rabbit meat from the bones, then shred it twice (see technique p. 44), making sure all of the small bones have been removed. Place in a bowl and stir in the parsley, chervil, and tarragon until well mixed. Taste and adjust the seasoning if needed. Spoon the rillettes into the terrine and cover with the pan juices. Cover and let set in the refrigerator for 24–36 hours.

TO SERVE

Serve on toasted country bread, topped with lightly dressed mesclun greens.

CHEFS' NOTES

To remove the fat more easily, chill the sauce so that the fat solidifies on the surface, then scoop it off using a spoon.

LA COCOTTE

TUNA RILLETTES WITH GREEN PEPPERCORNS

Rillettes de thon au poivre vert

Serves 4

Active time
25 minutes

Cooking time
5 minutes

Storage
3 days in the refrigerator

Equipment
Microplane grater
14-oz. (400-g) jar

Ingredients

20 green peppercorns
9 oz. (250 g) tuna packed in spring water, drained
1 tbsp (15 g) butter, softened
½ cup (4¼ oz./120 g) fromage frais
Finely grated zest and juice of 1 lemon
3½ tbsp (50 ml) olive oil
Salt and freshly ground pepper

To blanch the peppercorns, place in a saucepan with plenty of cold water and bring to a boil. Let simmer for 5 minutes, then drain and plunge into ice water to refresh.

Place the tuna in a mixing bowl and flake using a fork. Mix in the butter.

Season with salt and pepper and incorporate the fromage frais and lemon zest and juice. Stir in a few of the blanched peppercorns and reserve the rest for garnishing the rillettes just before serving. Spoon the rillettes into a jar to serve.

DUCK AND PARSNIP PARMENTIER

Parmentier de canard au panais et vin de noix

Serves 6

Active time

1 hour

Cooking time

2 hours

Storage

3–4 days in the refrigerator

Equipment

Fine-mesh sieve

Mandoline

Food processor

Disposable pastry bag

6 × 3-in. (8-cm) stainless steel rings, 3 in. (8 cm) deep

Ingredients

Braised duck

2 onions

1 carrot

3 duck legs

Olive oil

1¼ cups (300 ml) *vin de noix* (French walnut liqueur)

About 2 qt. (2 liters) white chicken stock (*fond blanc de volaille*)

Salt and freshly ground pepper

Parsnip slices

1 lb. (500 g) parsnips

7 tbsp (3½ oz./100 g) clarified butter

Parsnip puree

1 lb. (500 g) parsnips

5 tbsp (3 oz./80 g) butter

1½ tsp (7 g) salt

To serve

1 generous cup (3½ oz./100 g) ground pistachios

Mesclun greens, lightly dressed

PREPARING THE BRAISED DUCK

Preheat the oven to 350°F (180°C/Gas Mark 4). Peel and finely dice the onions and carrot. Cut the duck legs at the joints to separate the drumsticks from the thighs, then brown them in a Dutch oven over high heat with a little olive oil. Add the onions and carrots and cook until softened. Deglaze with the *vin de noix*, bring to a boil, and flambé. Add enough chicken stock to just cover the ingredients and bring to a boil again. Skim foam off the surface, cover, and place in the oven for 1½ hours, or until the meat easily falls off the bones. Drain the duck, reserving the pan juices. Remove the bones and shred the meat (see technique p. 44). Strain the pan juices through the fine-mesh sieve and reduce to a syrup-like consistency. Stir a small amount of the juices into the shredded duck and keep the rest for serving.

PREPARING THE PARSNIP SLICES

Peel and rinse the parsnips. Using the mandoline, cut them lengthwise into 15 very thin (1/16-in./2-mm) slices. Save the trimmings for the puree. Cook the slices on both sides in a skillet with the clarified butter until tender. Cut each slice into ¾ × 1½-in. (2 × 4-cm) rectangles.

PREPARING THE PARSNIP PUREE

Peel and rinse the parsnips and cook in a saucepan of boiling salted water with the trimmings from the parsnip slices. Drain and process to a puree in the food processor. Add the butter and salt and process until smooth. Adjust the seasonings if necessary. Transfer to the pastry bag and set aside at room temperature until ready to assemble.

ASSEMBLING THE PARMENTIERS

Place the stainless steel rings on a baking sheet lined with parchment paper. Line the rings with the parsnip slices and fill with alternating layers of parsnip puree and duck, finishing with the puree.

TO SERVE

Preheat the oven to 340°F (170°C/Gas Mark 3). Place the parmentiers in the oven for 10 minutes, or until heated through. Meanwhile, reheat the pan juices. Place each parmentier in a serving dish and remove the rings. Sprinkle with ground pistachios and spoon the pan juices around. Serve with mesclun greens.

GRILLONS CHARENTAIS

Serves 10

Active time
1½ hours

Resting time
4 hours

Cooking time
5½ hours

Cooling time
20 minutes

Chilling time
2 days

Storage
20 days in the refrigerator

Equipment
Instant-read thermometer
Ceramic or terra-cotta container of your choice
Muslin

Ingredients
1½ lb. (750 g) pork belly (*poitrine de porc*)
9 oz. (250 g) upper pork shoulder (*échine de porc*)
1 lb. 2 oz. (500 g) lower pork shoulder (*épaule de porc*)
¾ oz. (22 g) grey sea salt
1 bouquet garni
10½ oz. (300 g) lard
2 sprigs thyme
2 bay leaves
Scant ¾ cup (170 ml) water
2 cloves garlic
3½ oz. (100 g) grey shallots
½ tsp (2.5 g) ground white pepper
1 large pinch (0.7 g) quatre-épices spice mix
Scant ¼ tsp (1 g) ground nutmeg

Cut the pork belly and upper and lower shoulder meats into ¾-in. (2-cm) cubes. Season with the salt and place in a bowl with the bouquet garni. Cover and let rest in the refrigerator for 4 hours.

In a heavy-based Dutch oven, melt the lard over low heat. Increase the heat to medium-high and gradually add the meats. Cook for 20 minutes, stirring regularly, until browned. When the juices are clear, reduce the heat and spread the meat evenly across the base of the pan. Add the thyme, bay leaves, and water. Cover with a lid, leaving a slight opening, and cook at 185°F (85°C) for 2 hours, without stirring.

Peel and finely chop the garlic, removing the germs, and shallots and scatter over the meat. Season to taste with white pepper, quatre-épices, and nutmeg. Continue to cook for an additional 3 hours.

Using a skimmer, transfer the meat from the pan to your container, pressing it down lightly. Let cool for 20 minutes to room temperature, then chill. Warm the remaining cooking juices in the pan, strain through the muslin, and pour over the meat. Refrigerate for 2 days before serving.

STUFFED DISHES

STUFFED DUCK NECK WITH LANDES-STYLE FRIES AND EGGPLANT PUREE

Cou de canard farci, frites landaises et purée d'aubergine

Serves 6

Active time

2 hours

Marinating time

1 hour

Cooking time

About 3 hours

Storage

6 days in the refrigerator, after cooking

Equipment

Kitchen torch

Meat grinder + fine plate

Trussing needle and butcher's twine

Food processor

Deep fryer

Ingredients

Duck neck casings

6 duck necks

Scant ½ cup (100 ml) cognac

Farce

2 tbsp (15 g) shelled roasted pistachios

5 oz. (150 g) foie gras

4½ oz. (125 g) *lardo di Colonnata* (Italian cured pork fat)

7 oz. (200 g) duck leg

7 oz. (200 g) boneless pork shoulder (*échine de porc*)

2¾ tsp (14 g) salt per 2¼ lb. (1 kg) farce

3½ tsp (8 g) ground black pepper per 2¼ lb. (1 kg) farce

To cook the stuffed duck necks

10½ oz. (300 g) duck fat

Duck jus

7 oz. (200 g) shallots

6 duck necks

5 tbsp (3 oz./80 g) butter

3 sprigs thyme

Chinese five-spice powder

Salt and freshly ground pepper

Smoked eggplant puree

4 eggplants

2 tbsp (1 oz./30 g) sweet mustard (preferably Savora)

Olive oil

Finely grated zest of 1 lemon

Salt and freshly ground pepper

King trumpet mushrooms

5 king trumpet mushrooms

Clarified butter

Salt and freshly ground pepper

Landes-style fries

Neutral oil for deep-frying

4½ lb. (2 kg) potatoes

Generous ¾ cup (200 ml) duck fat

2 tbsp finely chopped parsley

Salt and coarsely ground pepper

To serve

½ head frisée lettuce

1 shallot, finely chopped

½ bunch chives, snipped

Scant ½ cup (100 ml) vinaigrette of your choice

PREPARING THE DUCK NECK CASINGS

Using the kitchen torch, singe any feathers off the duck necks. Remove the skin from the necks, taking care not to pierce it. Marinate the skin in the cognac for 1 hour. Drain, reserving the cognac for the farce.

PREPARING THE FARCE AND STUFFING THE NECKS

Preheat the oven to 300°F (150°C/Gas Mark 2) and toast the pistachios for 10 minutes. Cut the foie gras into ¾-in. (2-cm) dice and freeze. Cut the *lardo* into ¾-in. (2-cm) dice. Debone the duck leg and cut the pork shoulder into pieces. Grind the pork shoulder and duck meat together through the fine plate of the meat grinder into a bowl. Stir in the foie gras, *lardo*, pistachios, reserved cognac, salt, and pepper. Pat the casings dry with paper towel and sew the large ends closed using the trussing needle and twine. Carefully fill with farce, then close the smaller ends with a few stitches. If the skins split, cover in plastic wrap after stuffing and shape into uniform logs.

COOKING THE STUFFED DUCK NECKS

Preheat the oven to 285°F (140° C/Gas Mark 1). Place the stuffed duck necks in a Dutch oven with the duck fat, cover, and cook in the oven for 1 hour. Let cool in the fat.

PREPARING THE DUCK JUS

Peel and finely chop the shallots. Cut the duck necks crosswise into 1¼-in. (3-cm) slices and sauté with the butter in a skillet until deeply golden. Add the shallots and cook until translucent. Pour off excess fat, add the thyme and enough water to cover halfway. Cook for 30 minutes over low heat, skimming regularly. Strain and reduce until thick and syrupy. Season with the five-spice powder to taste, salt, and pepper.

PREPARING THE SMOKED EGGPLANT PUREE

Roast the eggplants over a gas burner until tender and charred, or roast in the oven at 350°F (180°C/Gas Mark 4) for 45 minutes. Cut in half and scoop the flesh into the food processor. Add the mustard, olive oil, and lemon zest and chop roughly. Season with salt and pepper.

PREPARING THE KING TRUMPET MUSHROOMS

Cut the mushrooms in half lengthwise and score with a criss-cross pattern (see photo). Sauté for 2 minutes on each side with a little clarified butter. Season with salt and pepper.

PREPARING THE LANDES-STYLE FRIES

Preheat the oil in the deep fryer to 320°F (160°C). Peel and rinse the potatoes, then cut them lengthwise into banana-shaped wedges about 4 in. (10 cm) long. Blanch in the hot oil, then finish cooking in the duck fat in a skillet, until golden. Season with the parsley, salt, and pepper.

TO SERVE

Toss the frisée, shallot, chives, and vinaigrette together. Caramelize the stuffed duck necks in a skillet with the duck fat they cooled in. Cut crosswise into 1½-in. (4-cm) slices. Spoon the jus onto serving plates and arrange the duck neck slices, eggplant puree, mushrooms, and salad on top. Serve with the fries on the side.

PIGS' TROTTERS STUFFED WITH VEAL SWEETBREADS

Pieds de cochon farcis aux ris de veau

Serves 10

Active time
3 hours

Cooking time
2½ hours

Equipment
Kitchen torch
Fine-mesh sieve
Food processor

Ingredients

Braised pigs' trotters
- 10 pigs' trotters
- 4 carrots, peeled and finely chopped
- 3 onions, peeled and finely chopped
- 1 bouquet garni
- Olive oil
- 2 qt. (2 liters) red wine
- 2 qt. (2 liters) veal stock
- 2 cups (500 ml) port wine
- 1 head garlic, cut in half crosswise
- 5 whole cloves
- 5 black peppercorns
- 1 oz. (30 g) black truffle bits *(brisures de truffe)*

Poultry farce
- 15 oz. (425 g) poultry breast meat of your choice
- 1 egg
- 7 tbsp (3½ oz./100 g) butter, softened
- 1 cup (250 ml) heavy cream, min. 35% fat
- Salt and freshly ground pepper

Veal sweetbreads
- 1 lb. (500 g) veal sweetbreads
- 7 tbsp (3½ oz./100 g) brown butter *(beurre noisette)*
- Salt and freshly ground pepper

To assemble
- 10½ oz. (300 g) pork caul fat, rinsed

To serve
- Parsley mashed potatoes
- Crisp potato fries
- Salad greens of your choice

PREPARING THE BRAISED PIGS' TROTTERS

Using the kitchen torch, singe off any remaining hairs on the trotters. Place the trotters in a large pan of salted water, bring to a boil, and blanch them for a few minutes. Drain and rinse under cold water. In a stockpot, cook the carrots and onions in a little olive oil with the bouquet garni over low heat for 5 minutes, until softened but not browned. Add the pigs' trotters and red wine, bring to a boil, then flambé. Add the veal stock and port wine, and return to a boil, skimming any foam from the surface. Add the garlic, cloves, and peppercorns, reduce the heat, and let simmer for about 2 hours. Lift out the trotters and remove the bones. Cover the trotters with plastic wrap and set aside. Strain the braising stock through the fine-mesh sieve and skim off the fat. In a saucepan, reduce the stock to a syrup. Adjust the seasonings and stir in the truffle bits.

PREPARING THE POULTRY FARCE

Dice the breast meat, place in the food processor with the egg, and process until smooth. Incorporate the butter, then pass the mixture through the fine-mesh sieve into a bowl. Place the bowl over a bed of ice and gradually fold in the cream using a spatula, taking care not to overmix.

PREPARING THE VEAL SWEETBREADS

Place the sweetbreads in a large pan of salted cold water, bring to a boil, and blanch them for 2 minutes. Drain and plunge them into a bowl of ice water to stop them cooking, then peel away the thin membranes. Cut the sweetbreads diagonally into 10 slices, each weighing about 2¾ oz. (80 g). Sauté the slices in a skillet with the brown butter until golden, and season with salt and pepper.

ASSEMBLING AND ROASTING THE STUFFED PIGS' TROTTERS

Preheat the oven to 350°F (180°C/Gas Mark 4). Cut the caul fat into 10 equal pieces. Fill the inside of each trotter with 1 tablespoon of farce, top with a sweetbread slice, then overwrap with a piece of caul fat. Fit the trotters snugly in a nonstick roasting pan and bake for about 20 minutes, depending on their size, until heated through and browned.

TO SERVE

Reheat the braising stock. Spoon a bed of parsley mashed potatoes into each serving bowl and place the trotters on top. Spoon over the stock and garnish with a few crisp fries and salad greens of your choice.

STUFFED QUAILS

Cailles farcies

Serves 4

Active time

3 hours

Cooking time

1¾ hours

Storage

5 days in the refrigerator

Equipment

Fine-mesh sieve

Trussing needle and butcher's twine

Meat netting

2 small flower-shaped cutters

Ingredients

Quails

4 quails (see Chefs' Notes)

Veal sweetbreads

1 lb. 2 oz. (500 g) veal sweetbreads

⅔ cup (150 ml) white vinegar

Quail jus

5 oz. (150 g) shallots

6 chicken wings

Quail carcasses (see above)

3½ tbsp (50 ml) peanut oil

5 unpeeled cloves garlic

1 sprig thyme

1 bay leaf

Scant ½ cup (100 ml) *vin jaune*

Croutons

1¼ lb. (600 g) sandwich bread

1 cup (250 ml) clarified butter, melted

Salt and freshly ground pepper

Stuffed quails

10½ oz. (300 g) cooked foie gras

2 qt. (2 liters) white chicken stock (*fond blanc de volaille*)

10 sheets gelatin (200 Bloom)

Salt and freshly ground pepper

To serve

3½ oz. (100 g) fine frisée

3½ oz. (100 g) mustard greens

¼ bunch chervil

1 oz. (30 g) truffle

5 oz. (150 g) large button mushrooms

16 leaves salad burnet

PREPARING THE QUAILS (see Chefs' Notes)

Using a small knife, debone the body cavities of the quails without cutting them open. Remove the giblets and roughly chop the carcasses for the jus.

PREPARING THE VEAL SWEETBREADS

To blanch the sweetbreads, place them in a large saucepan of cold salted water, add the vinegar, and bring to a boil. Let simmer for 10 minutes. Drain and peel away the thin membranes (see technique p. 50).

PREPARING THE QUAIL JUS

Peel and finely chop the shallots. Roughly chop the chicken wings. Brown the chopped wings and reserved chopped quail carcasses in a large saucepan with the peanut oil over medium-high heat. Add the shallots, garlic, thyme, and bay leaf, and deglaze with the *vin jaune*. Add enough water to just cover and simmer gently for 45 minutes. Strain through the fine-mesh sieve.

PREPARING THE CROUTONS

Cut the sandwich bread into 4 rectangles measuring 2 × 4 in. (5 × 10 cm) each. Cut out a small hollow in the center of each for the quails, leaving a ½-in. (1-cm) border. In a skillet, fry the bread in the clarified butter until golden all over. Season with salt and pepper and set aside.

STUFFING AND COOKING THE QUAILS

Cut the foie gras into 4 pieces and shape into small logs. Cut the sweetbreads lengthwise into 8 pieces. Cut 4 pieces of plastic wrap and place 1 foie gras log and 2 sweetbread pieces in each. Wrap and shape into cylinders. Season the insides of the quails with salt and pepper. Remove the plastic wrap from the foie gras and sweetbread logs and place one inside each quail. Using the trussing needle and twine, sew the quails up. Wrap in the meat netting and poach in the chicken stock for 45 minutes. Soak the gelatin in a bowl of cold water until softened. When the quails are done, remove their skin while still warm and place them on a rack. Squeeze the gelatin to remove excess water and stir it into the hot cooking juices until dissolved. Spoon the juices over the quails to glaze them, reserving a little for the flower decorations.

TO SERVE

Sort, wash, and spin dry the salad greens and chervil. Cut the truffle and mushrooms into very thin (1/16-in./2-mm) slices. Cut out flower shapes using the cookie cutters and quickly poach them in the quail cooking juices. Drain and arrange attractively over the quails. Garnish with the salad burnet leaves. Place each crouton on a serving plate, fill with salad greens and chervil, and set the quails on top.

CHEFS' NOTES

You can ask your butcher to prepare the quails.

PIGS' TROTTER AND FOIE GRAS CARPACCIO

Carpaccio de pieds de cochon et de foie gras

Serves 4

Active time
1½ hours

Cooking time
2 hours 50 minutes

Chilling time
2 hours

Storage
4 days in the refrigerator

Equipment
Razor
Steam oven (or steamer)
Fine-mesh sieve
Meat slicer

Ingredients

Pigs' trotters
4 pigs' trotters
7 oz. (200 g) carrots
10½ oz. (300 g) onions
5 whole cloves
1 bouquet garni
10 black peppercorns
1¼ cups (300 ml) white wine
Kosher salt
Salt and freshly ground pepper

Foie gras insert
1 lb. 2 oz. (500 g) cooked duck foie gras

To serve
4 tsp (20 ml) sherry vinegar
Baby greens
Pansy flowers
Salt and freshly ground pepper

PREPARING THE PIGS' TROTTERS

Using the razor, shave the hairs off the pigs' trotters. Rinse well, place in a large saucepan of cold salted water, and bring to a boil. Let simmer for 10 minutes, then drain and plunge into a bowl of ice water. Meanwhile, peel and finely chop the carrots. Peel the onions and stick them with the cloves. Drain the trotters, place in a saucepan of fresh water, and add the vegetables, bouquet garni, peppercorns, and wine. Season with kosher salt and cook at a boil for 2½ hours, until the meat easily detaches from the bones.

PREPARING THE FOIE GRAS INSERT

Devein the foie gras (see technique p. 48). Cut it into 4 pieces, each weighing approximately 4½ oz. (125 g), and cover separately with plastic wrap. Shape into 4 logs measuring 4 in. (10 cm) in diameter and 8 in. (20 cm) in length.

ASSEMBLING THE TROTTER AND FOIE GRAS ROLLS

Remove the trotters from the cooking liquid, reserving the liquid for the sauce. Carefully debone the trotters, keeping the skin intact. Arrange the trotters on a baking sheet, packing them closely together to make a rectangle. Place a weight on top to flatten them and chill for 2 hours. Preheat the steam oven to 185°F (85°C/Gas on lowest setting). Remove the plastic wrap from the foie gras logs and line them up end to end along one long side of the trotters. Using the plastic wrap, roll the trotters up tightly around the foie gras. Cut the roll into 4 pieces and cover each one in plastic wrap to hold the shape. Cook in the steam oven (or steam) for 10 minutes, then cool in the refrigerator or in a tray filled with ice water before slicing.

TO SERVE

Strain the trotter cooking liquid through the fine-mesh sieve into a saucepan and reduce it by half, until it has a syrup-like consistency. Stir in the sherry vinegar and season with salt and pepper. Using the meat slicer, cut the trotter rolls into ¼-in. (5-mm) slices. Arrange the slices in a rosette pattern on each serving plate. Serve lukewarm, garnished with baby greens and pansy flowers in the center, and add a few teardrops of reduced cooking liquid around the plate.

BEEF AND CARROT STEW-STYLE STUFFED SQUID

Calamars farcis cuisinés comme un bœuf carotte

Serves 10

Active time

1 hour

Cooking time

3½ hours

Storage

2 days in the refrigerator, after stuffing and cooking

Equipment

Fine-mesh sieve

Disposable pastry bag

Wooden toothpicks

Mandoline

Ingredients

Braised oxtail

3½ lb. (1.5 kg) oxtail (*queues de boeuf*)

3 tbsp (1¾ oz./50 g) butter

3½ tbsp (50 ml) neutral oil

2 carrots, chopped

2 onions, chopped

2 stalks celery, chopped

2 bay leaves

3 sprigs thyme

2 cups (500 ml) red wine

About 2 qt. (2 liters) water

Salt and freshly ground pepper

Oxtail farce

Oxtail pan juices

2 tbsp (30 g) *moutarde violette de Brive* (Brive violet mustard)

2 tbsp chopped shallot

2 tbsp chopped parsley

Stuffed squid

10 medium squid (4–5 in./10–12 cm long)

Olive oil

Carrot relish

14 oz. (400 g) carrots

2 shallots

Butter

Generous ¾ cup (200 ml) carrot juice

1¾ oz. (50 g) fresh ginger, peeled and finely chopped

1 tbsp (15 g) Meaux mustard

¼ bunch chives, snipped

Salt and freshly ground pepper

Garnishes

30 pearl onions, peeled

2 tbsp (1 oz./30 g) butter

1 tbsp (15 g) sugar

2 carrots

3½ oz. (100 g) thick bacon

Canola oil

To serve

Olive oil

Generous ¾ cup (200 ml) oxtail pan juices, warm

A few blood dock leaves

Pea shoots

PREPARING THE BRAISED OXTAIL AND OXTAIL FARCE (1 DAY AHEAD)

Preheat the oven to 350°F (180°C/Gas Mark 4). Separate the oxtail at the joints and brown in a Dutch oven with the butter and oil. Add the carrots, onions, celery, bay leaves, and thyme and cook until softened. Deglaze with the red wine, then add water to just cover the meat and vegetables. Season with salt and pepper. Skim foam off the surface, cover, and place in the oven for 2½ hours, until the meat easily falls off the bones. Drain the oxtail, reserving the pan juices. Remove the bones and shred the meat. Strain the juices through the fine-mesh sieve and reduce further if necessary. Add half the pan juices and the *moutarde violette* to the shredded oxtail meat and stir in the chopped shallot and parsley. Adjust the seasonings and transfer to the pastry bag.

PREPARING THE STUFFED SQUID

To remove the head and tentacles from the squid, slowly pull out the quill inside the body, taking care not to pierce it or the ink sac. Remove the skin and rinse the bodies under cold water. Cut off the tentacles, rinse, and reserve. Pipe the farce into the bodies and close the ends with toothpicks, making sure to leave a 1¼ in. (3 cm) space between the farce and the toothpick.

PREPARING THE CARROT RELISH

Peel and cut the carrots into 1/16-in. (2-mm) dice. Peel and finely chop the shallots. In a skillet, cook the carrots and shallots with a little butter until softened but not browned. Add the carrot juice and ginger, cover, and cook over low heat until the liquid has evaporated completely. Stir in the mustard and chives, adjust the seasonings, and keep warm.

PREPARING THE GARNISHES

Cook the pearl onions in a sauté pan with the butter, sugar, and ½ in. (1 cm) of water, until the onions absorb the liquid and the butter and sugar caramelize. Peel and slice the carrots lengthwise into very thin (1/16 in./2 mm) strips using the mandoline. Blanch the strips in boiling salted water for 2 minutes. Drain and plunge into a bowl of ice water. Cut the bacon into ¼ × ¾-in. (0.5 × 2-cm) pieces, place in a saucepan of cold water, and bring to a boil. Drain and refresh in ice water, then sauté in a skillet with a little canola oil.

TO SERVE

Preheat the oven to 350°F (180°C/Gas Mark 4). Brown the stuffed squid on both sides in an oven-safe skillet with a little olive oil. Place in the oven for 8 minutes to finish cooking. Remove the toothpicks and trim the ends of the squid neatly. Sear the tentacles with a little olive oil over high heat for 3 minutes. Spoon a little carrot relish onto each plate and top with the stuffed squid. Drizzle with the warm pan juices, then arrange the tentacles, carrot ribbons, pearl onions, and bacon attractively around the plate. Garnish with blood dock leaves and pea shoots.

SPICY CABBAGE AND HERB SAUSAGES

Saucisses au vert

Serves 4

Active time
2 hours

Cooking time
1¾ hours

Soaking time
15 minutes

Chilling time
2 hours

Storage
3 days in the refrigerator

Equipment
Immersion blender
Microplane grater
Manual sausage stuffer
Butcher's twine
Blender
Sausage pricker

Ingredients

Sausages
- 1 pointed (sweetheart) cabbage
- ½ green cabbage
- 10½ oz. (300 g) kale
- Scant ½ cup (3½ oz./100 g) pearl barley
- ¾ cup (5¼ oz./150 g) split peas
- Finely grated zest of 1 lime
- Scant ⅓ cup (1¾ oz./50 g) kasha (toasted buckwheat groats)
- ½ bunch flat-leaf parsley, finely chopped
- ⅓ oz. (10 g) fresh horseradish, peeled
- ⅓ oz. (10 g) fresh ginger, peeled
- 3 ft. (1 meter) natural casing, 24/26 mm, cleaned (see technique p. 52)
- Coarse grey sea salt and freshly ground pepper

Green jalapeño sauce
- ⅔ oz. (20 g) pickled jalapeños
- 4 tsp (20 ml) olive oil
- Scant ½ cup (100 ml) heavy cream, min 35% fat
- 1 sweet green vegetable chili pepper (*piment végétal*), chopped
- Juice of 1 lemon
- Scant ½ tsp (1 g) xanthan gum

To serve
- 3½ tbsp (50 ml) olive oil

PREPARING THE SAUSAGES

Remove the outer leaves from the pointed and green cabbages and cut out the cores. Separate the leaves of the cabbages and kale, remove the ribs, and rinse. Bring a large saucepan of cold water to a boil and season with coarse grey sea salt. Blanch the cabbages and kale separately in the boiling water for 8 minutes, then drain and plunge into ice water. Drain on paper towel and chop finely. Simmer the pearl barley in a covered pan over medium-low heat for about 30 minutes, until tender but still slightly chewy, then drain. Place the split peas in a saucepan with twice their volume of cold water, bring to a boil, and simmer for about 25 minutes until soft. Process with the immersion blender until smooth, then dry out in a saucepan over low heat; this will serve as a binder. To make the farce, combine the cabbages and kale, pearl barley, and split pea puree in a bowl, then add the lime zest, kasha, and parsley. Using the Microplane grater, grate in the horseradish and ginger. Season with salt and pepper and stir to combine. Soak the casings in lukewarm water for 15 minutes. Slide one end of the clean casing onto the filling tube of the sausage stuffer. Crank the stuffer to fill the casing, holding it to ensure even distribution of the farce and avoid air bubbles. To shape the sausage links, pinch the filled casing at about 4-in. (10-cm) intervals and twist two or three times (see technique p. 110). Tie each end with pieces of twine. Chill for 2 hours.

PREPARING THE GREEN JALAPEÑO SAUCE

Remove the seeds from the jalapeños, place in a saucepan of cold water, and bring to a boil. Drain, then sweat briefly in a skillet with the olive oil. Add the cream and bring to a boil. Pour into the blender and add the sweet chili pepper, lemon juice, and xanthan gum, to thicken the sauce. Process until smooth and place in a bowl over ice.

TO SERVE

Using the sausage pricker, pierce all over to eliminate air bubbles. Gently brown the string of sausages in a skillet with the olive oil (take care as they are quite fragile) for about 15 minutes.

GINGER AND LEMONGRASS CRÉPINETTES

Crépinette au gingembre et à la citronnelle

Serves 4

Active time
1 hour

Cooking time
30 minutes

Storage
2 days in the refrigerator

Equipment
Meat grinder + medium plate

Ingredients

Crépinettes
- 1¼ lb. (600 g) pork shoulder (*échine de porc*)
- 7 oz. (200 g) pork fatback (*lard gras*)
- 1 onion, finely chopped
- 2 tbsp (30 ml) olive oil
- 1¼ cups (300 ml) dry white wine
- 1 tbsp finely chopped peeled fresh ginger
- 1 tbsp finely chopped lemongrass
- 1 tbsp finely chopped fresh cilantro
- 2¾ tsp (14 g) salt per 2¼ lb. (1 kg) farce
- 3½ tsp (8 g) ground Voatsiperifery pepper per 2¼ lb. (1 kg) farce
- 7 oz. (200 g) pork caul fat, rinsed

Wilted spinach
- 1¾ lb. (800 g) fresh spinach
- 5 tbsp (2½ oz./70 g) butter
- Salt and freshly ground pepper

Sauce
- 3½ tbsp (50 ml) olive oil
- Generous ¾ cup (200 ml) sweet soy sauce
- 3 tbsp (1¾ oz./50 g) butter

To serve
- 1 tsp (3 g) buckwheat groats (kasha)
- 1 oz. (30 g) baby spinach

PREPARING THE CRÉPINETTES

Cut the pork shoulder and fatback into pieces and grind through the meat grinder into a bowl. In a skillet, cook the onion with the olive oil over medium-low heat until softened but not browned. Deglaze the pan with the white wine and reduce until the onions are completely soft and all the liquid has evaporated. Let cool completely, then stir into the ground meat. Add the ginger, lemongrass, cilantro, salt, and pepper and stir to combine without overmixing. Shape into 4 balls, each weighing 5¼ oz. (150 g), then flatten into disks. Cut the caul fat into 4 equal squares and wrap around the disks, enclosing them completely. Chill until cooking.

PREPARING THE WILTED SPINACH

De-stem and wash the spinach leaves, then spin dry. Melt the butter in a sauté pan over medium heat, add the spinach, and cook until wilted. Season with salt and pepper and keep warm.

COOKING THE CRÉPINETTES AND PREPARING THE SAUCE

Preheat the oven to 350°F (180°C/Gas Mark 4). Heat the olive oil in an oven-safe nonstick skillet over medium-high heat, add the crépinettes, and brown them on both sides. Place the pan in the oven for 8 minutes to finish cooking. Remove the crépinettes from the pan, skim the fat off the pan juices, and add the soy sauce. Bring to a boil, then stir in the butter until melted. Return the crépinettes to the pan to coat them with the sauce.

TO SERVE

Place each crépinette over a bed of wilted spinach, sprinkle with buckwheat groats, and garnish with baby spinach leaves.

SCALLOP AND VEGETABLE "HOT-AIR BALLOONS" WITH CHAMPAGNE SAUCE

Montgolfière de Saint-Jacques, petits légumes et sauce champagne

Serves 4

Active time
35 minutes

Cooking time
15–20 minutes

Chilling time
20 minutes

Freezing time
15 minutes

Equipment
Fine-mesh sieve
4 lion's head (small, deep, ovenproof) soup bowls

Ingredients

Scallop and vegetable filling
3½ oz. (100 g) button mushrooms
Butter
Olive oil
3½ oz. (100 g) broccoli
3 oz. (80 g) celeriac
3 oz. (80 g) green asparagus
3½ oz. (100 g) baby carrots, tops on
2 oz. (60 g) thin French green beans
12 scallops (about 1 lb./480 g)
Salt and freshly ground pepper

Champagne sauce
2 oz. (60 g) tomatoes
3½ oz. (100 g) shallots
1 tbsp (15 g) butter
1½ tbsp (15 g) flour
1⅔ cups (400 ml) champagne
Generous ¾ cup (200 ml) white chicken stock (*fond blanc de volaille*)
¼ cup (1½ oz./40 g) crème fraîche

To assemble
9 oz. (250 g) quick puff pastry (see technique p. 58)
1 generous tbsp (12 g) toasted sesame seeds
1 egg
2 egg yolks

To garnish (optional)
Shaved white truffle

PREPARING THE SCALLOP AND VEGETABLE FILLING

Wash and quarter the mushrooms and brown them in a skillet over medium-high heat with a little butter and olive oil. Season with salt and pepper. Wash the broccoli, remove the florets, and cut the most tender parts of the stalks into small dice. Peel the celeriac and cut into ½ × 1¼-in. (1 × 3-cm) sticks. Cut off the asparagus tips ¾ in. (2 cm) from the ends (reserve the tips for another use) and cut 1¼ in. (3 cm) off the bases (discard). Cut each remaining stalk into 4 diagonal pieces. Wash and scrub the carrots and cut off the tops, leaving ½ in. (1 cm). Trim the ends off the green beans. Poach all the vegetables (except the mushrooms) for a few seconds in a large saucepan of boiling salted water and plunge into ice-cold water to stop the cooking. In a skillet with a little olive oil and butter, cook the vegetables separately over medium-high heat until lightly golden. Season with salt and pepper, then chill until assembling. In a clean skillet with a pat of butter, brown the scallops on one side over high heat for 1 minute, then place in the freezer for 15–20 minutes to prevent them from over-cooking in the oven.

PREPARING THE CHAMPAGNE SAUCE

Wash and cut the tomatoes (skin on) into ½-in. (1-cm) dice. Peel and finely chop the shallots and cook in the butter over low heat until softened. Stir in the flour and tomatoes. Pour in the champagne and reduce by half. Add the stock and let cook for about 10 minutes, then stir in the crème fraîche and cook over low heat until the sauce coats the back of a spoon. Strain through the fine-mesh sieve into a bowl, pressing down to recover all the liquid.

ASSEMBLING THE "HOT AIR BALLOONS"

Preheat the oven to 450°F (240°C/Gas Mark 8). Roll the pastry to a thickness of 1⁄16 in. (1.5 mm) and cut out 4 disks with a diameter about ¾ in. (2 cm) greater than that of the soup bowls. Divide the vegetables between the bowls and sprinkle with sesame seeds. Add 3 scallops and about ¼ cup (2 oz./60 g) of champagne sauce to each bowl. Whisk together the egg and egg yolks to make an egg wash and brush around the edges of each pastry disk, making a ¾-in. (1.5-cm) border. Place the disks over the bowls with the egg wash side down. Gently press down around the edges to seal the pastry to the bowls. Brush the tops with egg wash, poke a small hole in the center of each one to let steam escape, and score decoratively with a fine-tipped knife. Place in the oven, reduce the temperature to 430°F (220°C/Gas Mark 7), and bake for 20 minutes, until the pastry is puffed and golden brown. Serve immediately, garnished with shaved white truffle, if you wish.

MARENGO-STYLE POULTRY PAUPIETTES

Paupiettes de volaille marengo

Serves 4

Active time
2 hours

Cooking time
1 hour

Storage
3 days in the refrigerator, before cooking

Equipment
Food processor
Fine-mesh drum sieve
Butcher's twine
Fine-mesh sieve

Ingredients

Poultry paupiettes
4 deboned chicken legs
10½ oz. (300 g) poultry breast meat of your choice
¼ cup (2 oz./60 g) egg white (about 2 whites)
5 tbsp (3 oz./80 g) butter, softened
⅔ cup (150 ml) heavy cream, min. 35% fat
8 slices smoked bacon
9 oz. (250 g) caul fat, rinsed
12 bay leaves
Salt and freshly ground pepper

Vegetables
20 potatoes
10½ oz. (300 g) button mushrooms
2 tbsp (1 oz./30 g) brown butter (*beurre noisette*)
10½ oz. (300 g) pearl onions, peeled
3 tbsp (1¾ oz./50 g) butter
1¼ tsp (5 g) sugar
Salt and freshly ground pepper

Marengo sauce
1 onion
4 cloves garlic
2 tbsp (20 g) flour
Scant ½ cup (100 ml) peanut oil
1 tbsp (20 g) butter
⅔ cup (150 ml) white wine
2 tbsp (1 oz./30 g) tomato paste
About 4 cups (1 liter) clear brown veal stock (*fond brun de veau clair*)
1 bouquet garni
Salt and freshly ground pepper

To serve
Pea shoots

PREPARING THE POULTRY PAUPIETTES

Using a rolling pin, flatten the chicken legs between two sheets of parchment paper. Remove the tendons from the breast meat and cut into pieces. Place in the food processor with the egg whites and a little salt and process until smooth. Incorporate the butter. Pass the mixture through the drum sieve into a large bowl set over a bed of ice. Stir in the cream. Season the insides of the legs, skin side down, and stuff with the breast mixture. Shape into spheres and wrap 2 bacon slices around each. Cut the caul fat into 4 equal pieces and wrap around the paupiettes. Top each with 3 bay leaves and tie at regular intervals with butcher's twine, crossing the twine over the center of each paupiette to resemble the ridges of a melon.

PREPARING THE VEGETABLES

Peel the potatoes and cut them into 3-in. (8-cm) cylinders, about ¾ in. (2 cm) in diameter. Blanch in a saucepan of boiling salted water until almost tender. Peel, wash, and dice the mushrooms. Sauté them in a skillet with the brown butter until tender and season with salt and pepper. In a separate saucepan, sweat the pearl onions with the regular butter, cooking until the liquid has evaporated. Add the sugar and let caramelize.

PREPARING THE MARENGO SAUCE

Preheat the oven to 350°F (180°C/Gas Mark 4). Peel and finely chop the onion and garlic, removing the germs. Coat the paupiettes in the flour and pan-fry in an oven-safe skillet with the peanut oil and butter until golden. Remove from the pan and wipe out excess fat with paper towel. Sweat the onions in the same skillet and deglaze with the white wine. Let reduce, then stir in the tomato paste. Return the paupiettes to the pan, pour in enough stock to cover, and bring to a boil. Add the garlic and bouquet garni, cover, and cook in the oven for 30 minutes. Remove the paupiettes and strain the sauce through the fine-mesh sieve, pressing down to extract all the juices. Return to the pan and adjust the seasonings and consistency if necessary. Place the paupiettes in the sauce, add the vegetables, and let simmer for about 10 minutes.

TO SERVE

Remove the twine from the paupiettes and serve in soup plates surrounded by the potato cylinders and Marengo sauce. Garnish with pea shoots.

COUNTRY-STYLE STUFFED TOMATOES WITH SALAD TARTLETS

Tomate farcie champêtre, salade mêlée

Serves 4

Active time

1 hour

Cooking time

2 hours

Storage

2 days in the refrigerator

Equipment

Fine-mesh sieve

4-in. (10-cm) round cutter

8 × 3-in. (8-cm) tartlet pans

Ingredients

Tomatoes and pork cheek and pigs' trotter stuffing

4 large yellow or orange beefsteak tomatoes

1 onion

7 oz. (200 g) carrots

6 pork cheeks

1 sprig thyme

1 bay leaf

1 bunch flat-leaf parsley

1 bunch scallions

2 cooked pigs' trotters (*pieds de cochon*), juices reserved (whether cooking the trotters yourself or using ones from a can or jar)

2/3 cup (150 ml) white wine

3 shallots

Salt

Salad tartlets

5¼ oz. (150 g) mizuna

5¼ oz. (150 g) thin yellow frisée

¼ bunch chervil

4 sheets brik pastry

3½ tbsp (50 ml) melted clarified butter

To assemble

Scant ½ cup (1¾ oz./50 g) bread crumbs

Reduced pork cheek cooking liquid

4 tsp (20 ml) apple cider vinegar

4 tsp (20 ml) walnut oil

1 scallion, sliced diagonally

Salt and freshly ground pepper

PREPARING THE TOMATOES AND PORK CHEEK AND PIGS' TROTTER STUFFING

Wash the tomatoes, slice off the tops, and scoop out the seeds and pulp. Season the insides with salt and turn upside down to drain. Peel and finely chop the onion and carrots. Peel the membranes off the pork cheeks. Place the cheeks in a large saucepan of cold salted water and bring to a boil. Add the onion, carrots, thyme, and bay leaf and simmer gently for 1 hour. Meanwhile, finely chop the parsley and thinly slice the scallions. Debone the trotters, roughly chop the meat, and place in a skillet over medium-high heat with the parsley, scallions, and reserved juices. Sauté until browned, then deglaze the pan with the white wine and let reduce. Set aside. Drain the pork cheeks, reserve the liquid, and cut the meat into approximately ½-in. (1-cm) pieces. Peel and finely chop the shallots and place in a skillet with the cheeks and a little of their cooking liquid. Cook over low heat for about 20 minutes, until reduced with the texture of a compote, then stir in the trotter mixture. Strain the reserved pork cheek cooking liquid through the fine-mesh sieve into a saucepan and reduce to a syrupy consistency. Set aside.

PREPARING THE TARTLETS

Preheat the oven to 300°F (150°C/Gas Mark 2). Wash the salad leaves and herbs and spin them dry. Using the cutter, cut out four 4-in. (10-cm) disks of brik pastry. Brush with the clarified butter and bake each one between two tartlet pans for 5 minutes, until the pastry is golden and crisp.

ASSEMBLING THE DISH

Preheat the oven to 300°F (150°C/Gas Mark 2). Fill the tomatoes with the stuffing, sprinkle with bread crumbs, and replace the tops. Brush with a little reduced pork cheek cooking liquid and bake for 20 minutes. Stir the cider vinegar into the remaining cooking liquid. Toss the greens with the walnut oil and season with salt and pepper. Divide between the tartlet cases. Place a stuffed tomato on each serving plate and decorate with scallion slices. Add a salad tartlet and serve with the reduced cooking liquid.

STUFFED CONCHIGLIONI

Conchiglioni farcis

Serves 5 as a main course or 8 as an appetizer

Active time
30 minutes

Cooking time
1 hour

Storage
3 days in the refrigerator

Ingredients

Pigs' trotter stuffing

- 14½ oz. (440 g) cooked pigs' trotters (*pieds de cochon*), juices reserved (whether cooking the trotters yourself or using ones from a can or jar)
- 3½ oz. (100 g) shallots
- ⅓ oz. (10 g) garlic
- 1 tbsp (20 g) butter, divided
- Scant 1 cup (240 ml) white wine
- 1½ oz. (40 g) flat-leaf parsley
- 8½ oz. (240 g) celeriac

Tomato sauce

- 2¾ lb. (1.2 kg) tomatoes
- 4½ oz. (130 g) onion
- ¼ oz. (8 g) garlic
- 3½ tbsp (50 ml) olive oil
- Fresh thyme, to taste
- Bay leaves, to taste
- Salt

To assemble

- ⅓ cup (2 oz./60 g) grated Parmesan
- 40 conchiglioni pasta shells (about 1¼ lb./575 g)

To garnish

- Fresh basil leaves

PREPARING THE PIGS' TROTTER STUFFING

Preheat the oven to 250°F (120°C/Gas Mark ½). Place the pigs' trotters and juices in a Dutch oven, cover, and heat in the oven for 20 minutes, or until the meat easily detaches from the bones. Remove the bones and place the trotters flat in a dish. Cover with plastic wrap and let cool completely in the refrigerator. Peel and finely chop the shallots and garlic. Cook the shallots with half the butter in a skillet over low heat until softened, then add the garlic and cook for an additional 5 minutes. Deglaze with the white wine, then reduce until all the liquid has evaporated. Transfer to a bowl, cover with plastic wrap, and chill until assembling. Wash and finely chop the parsley and chill covered with plastic wrap. Peel the celeriac and finely dice into brunoise (see technique p. 38). Cook in a skillet with the remaining butter over low heat for 10 minutes, until just tender. When the pigs' trotters are cold, cut them into approximately ⅛-in. (4-mm) dice. Transfer to a bowl, cover with plastic wrap, and chill until assembling.

PREPARING THE TOMATO SAUCE

Peel the tomatoes, remove the seeds, and cut into ½-in. (1-cm) dice. Peel and finely chop the onion, then peel, remove the germs, and finely chop the garlic. Cook the onion with the oil in a sauté pan over low heat until softened, then add the garlic. Add the tomatoes, thyme and bay leaves to taste, and a pinch of salt. Let cook over low heat, covered, for 30–40 minutes, stirring occasionally, until thick and jammy. Taste and correct the seasonings as needed.

ASSEMBLING THE STUFFED SHELLS

Preheat the oven to 285°F (140°C/Gas Mark 1). Combine the diced pigs' trotters, celeriac, and shallot mixture in a sauté pan and cook, stirring gently, until heated through. Remove from the heat, stir in the Parmesan and chilled parsley, and adjust the seasonings if needed. Cook the pasta in boiling salted water until al dente (12–15 minutes, or according to the package instructions). Drain and rinse under cold water to stop the cooking. Spread half the tomato sauce across the base of a baking dish, then stuff the shells with the pigs' trotter mixture and place over the sauce. Cover with aluminum foil and bake for 15 minutes.

TO SERVE

Warm the remaining tomato sauce and divide between serving bowls. Arrange the shells over the sauce and garnish with a few basil leaves.

COOKED CHARCUTERIE

HAM SALAD WITH POACHED EGG AND SPICED SABAYON

Salade de jambonneau, œuf poché et sabayon aux épices

Serves 6

Active time
45 minutes

Cooking time
30 minutes

Storage
2 days in the refrigerator

Equipment
Instant-read thermometer

Ingredients

Ham salad
- 1¾ lb. (800 g) cooked boneless ham, preferably knuckle (*jambonneau*)
- 1 shallot
- 3½ tbsp (50 ml) cornichons
- 3½ oz. (100 g) sundried tomatoes
- 2½ tbsp (20 g) capers
- 1 bunch chives, snipped
- 1 tbsp finely chopped fresh tarragon
- Scant ½ cup (100 ml) olive oil
- 1 generous tbsp (20 g) Dijon mustard
- 3½ tbsp (50 ml) balsamic vinegar
- Salt and freshly ground pepper

Poached eggs
- 4 cups (1 liter) water
- Scant ½ cup (100 ml) white vinegar
- 6 eggs

Spiced sabayon
- 2 egg yolks
- 2 tbsp (30 ml) water
- 1 stick plus 2 tsp (4½ oz./125 g) clarified butter, melted
- ½ tsp (1 g) ground Voatsiperifery pepper
- ½ tsp (1 g) *piment d'Espelette*
- Salt

To serve
- 9 hard-boiled quail eggs, peeled and halved
- 1 red onion, finely sliced
- A few chickweed leaves

PREPARING THE HAM SALAD

Cut the ham into ¼-in. (5-mm) dice. Peel and finely chop the shallot. Finely chop the cornichons and sundried tomatoes. Place everything in a bowl and add the capers, chives, tarragon, oil, mustard, and vinegar. Season with salt and pepper and toss until well combined.

PREPARING THE POACHED EGGS

Bring the water and vinegar to a simmer in a wide pan. Fill a bowl with ice water. Poach the eggs in the simmering water for 3–4 minutes, until the whites are just set. Drain using a skimmer and plunge them into the ice water to stop the cooking.

PREPARING THE SPICED SABAYON

Place the egg yolks and water in a small saucepan. Whisking briskly, cook over low heat or a bain-marie, until foamy and thick. Ensure the temperature does not exceed 150°F (65°C), or the eggs will begin to scramble. Whisk in the clarified butter, a little at a time, then whisk in the pepper, *piment d'Espelette*, and salt to taste. Keep warm in a bain-marie or other warm place.

TO SERVE

If you wish, reheat the poached eggs in a warm-water bath. Place a little ham salad on each serving plate, top with a poached egg, and drizzle with a little spiced sabayon. Garnish with the quail eggs, a few red onion slices, and chickweed leaves.

SAVORY MUSTARD-GLAZED HAM CAKE

Jambonneau glacé à la moutarde

Serves 6

Active time
3 hours

Chilling time
5 hours + overnight

Cooking time
2½ hours

Storage
5 days in the refrigerator

Equipment
Fine-mesh sieve

8-in. (20-cm) round cake pan, 6 in. (15 cm) deep

Ingredients

Ham

2 lightly salted uncooked hams, preferably shanks (*jambonneaux demi-sel arrière*)

2 carrots

1 onion

1 bouquet garni

3 whole cloves

5 black peppercorns

Blood sausage and chestnut layer

10½ oz. (300 g) cooked blood sausage (*boudin noir*)

9 oz. (250 g) cooked chestnuts

Mustard glaze

6 sheets gelatin (200 Bloom)

1⅓ cups (7 oz./200 g) mustard seeds

2½ tbsp (2 oz./50 g) honey

Scant ½ cup (100 ml) apple cider vinegar

3½ tsp (10 g) ground turmeric

⅓ cup (3 oz./80 g) Savora mustard

Salt and freshly ground pepper

To serve

10½ oz. (300 g) ground pistachios

PREPARING THE HAM

To blanch the hams, place them in a large saucepan of cold salted water and bring to a boil. Meanwhile, peel and finely chop the carrots and onion. Drain the ham, return to a saucepan of fresh water, then add the vegetables, bouquet garni, cloves, and peppercorns. Cook at a gentle simmer until the meat easily detaches from the bones (about 2 hours).

PREPARING THE BLOOD SAUSAGE AND CHESTNUT LAYER

Remove the casing from the blood sausage and roll the sausage into a 6-in. (15-cm) disk between two sheets of parchment paper. Chill until assembling. Roughly chop the cooked chestnuts.

ASSEMBLING THE CAKE

Remove the ham from the saucepan, reserving the cooking liquid. Carefully remove the bones and skin and set the skin aside. Cut the ham into pieces. Strain the cooking liquid through the fine-mesh sieve into a saucepan and reduce by half. Line the base of the cake pan with one of the pieces of ham skin (with the outer side facing down) and arrange pieces of ham over it, making an approximately 1¼-in. (3-cm) layer. Top with the blood sausage layer and scatter the chestnuts over it. Cover with another layer of ham and then with the second piece of ham skin (with the outer side facing up). Pour a little of the reduced cooking liquid into the pan and press plastic wrap over the surface. Place a weight on top to press down gently. Chill for 5 hours.

PREPARING THE MUSTARD GLAZE

Soak the gelatin in a bowl of cold water until softened. To blanch the mustard seeds, place them in a saucepan of cold water, bring to a boil, and drain. Repeat twice more. In a separate saucepan, bring the honey and vinegar to a boil, then stir in the turmeric and sweet mustard. Remove from the heat, season with salt and pepper, and stir in the blanched mustard seeds. Squeeze the gelatin to remove excess water and stir into the mixture until dissolved. Let cool to lukewarm.

GLAZING THE CAKE

Turn the cake out of the mold and pour the lukewarm glaze over it. Spread into an even layer over the top. Chill overnight to let the glaze set.

TO SERVE

Coat the sides with the ground pistachios, cut into wedges, and serve.

BLOOD SAUSAGE EMPANADAS WITH TARBAIS BEAN HUMMUS AND PIQUILLO COULIS

Ravioles de boudin noir frits, houmous de tarbais et coulis de piquillos

Serves 10

Active time

1 hour

Chilling time

1 hour

Cooking time

About 1 hour

Equipment

Stand mixer + dough hook

Pasta maker

4-in. (10-cm) round cookie cutter

Disposable pastry bag

Food processor

Food processor with a heating element (e.g. Thermomix, optional)

Fine-mesh sieve

Deep fryer

Instant-read thermometer

Ingredients

Empanada dough

1⅔ cups (7 oz./200 g) all-purpose flour

2 eggs

2 tbsp (30 ml) olive oil

2 pinches salt

Blood sausage filling

14 oz. (400 g) blood sausage *(boudin noir)*

3½ tbsp (50 ml) heavy cream, min. 35% fat

1 pinch *piment d'Espelette*

Tarbais bean hummus

9 oz. (250 g) cooked Tarbais beans

½ clove garlic, peeled

2 tbsp (1 oz./30 g) tahini

½ tsp (2 g) ground cumin

3½ tbsp (50 ml) olive oil

Piquillo pepper coulis

7 oz. (200 g) piquillo peppers, from a jar

3½ tbsp (50 ml) olive oil

Scant ½ tsp (2 g) salt

2 tsp (5 g) *piment d'Espelette*

Parsley oil

1¾ oz. (50 g) flat-leaf parsley

½ clove garlic, peeled

½ tsp (3 g) salt

Scant ½ cup (100 ml) grape-seed oil

To cook and serve

Oil for deep-frying

10 slices blood sausage (about 2 sausages)

10 pickled guindilla peppers

Pea shoots

Tarbais beans

CHEFS' NOTES

Wonton wrappers can be used instead of making the empanada dough yourself.

PREPARING THE EMPANADA DOUGH

Knead together the flour, eggs, oil, and salt in the stand mixer, or by hand, until smooth. Shape the dough into a ball, cover with plastic wrap, and chill for 1 hour. Pass the dough through the pasta maker several times, starting on the widest setting and gradually lowering it to setting 6. Lay the dough flat and cut out thirty 4-in. (10-cm) disks using the cutter. Chill on a baking sheet until ready to use.

PREPARING THE BLOOD SAUSAGE FILLING

Remove the casings from the sausage. Place the sausage meat in a bowl and mash in the cream and *piment d'Espelette* using a fork. Transfer to the pastry bag. Brush a little water over the edges of the dough disks to moisten them. Pipe a little filling in the center of each disk, then fold in half to enclose the filling. Pinch the edges to seal well and chill until cooking.

PREPARING THE TARBAIS BEAN HUMMUS

Place the beans, garlic, tahini, and cumin in the food processor and process until smooth. With the motor running, gradually add the olive oil until emulsified. Chill until serving.

PREPARING THE PIQUILLO PEPPER COULIS

Process the piquillo peppers with the olive oil, salt, and *piment d'Espelette* until smooth. Chill until serving.

PREPARING THE PARSLEY OIL

Combine the parsley, garlic, salt, and oil in the food processor with a heating element. Cook for 40 minutes at 160°F (70°C) on speed 2. Strain through the fine-mesh sieve and chill until serving. Alternatively, if you do not have a food processor with a heating element, place the ingredients in an oven-safe pan, cover, and cook in the oven at 160°F (70°C/Gas on lowest setting) for 40 minutes. Chop finely in the food processor, then strain and chill.

TO COOK AND SERVE

Preheat the oven to 430°F (220°C/Gas Mark 7) with the broiler on. Heat the oil for deep-frying to 355°F (180°C). Deep-fry the empanadas until lightly golden, without crowding them (cook in batches, if necessary). Drain on paper towel and season with salt. Cut the blood sausage crosswise into 10 slices, 1¼ in. (3 cm) thick. Place on a baking sheet, brush with olive oil, and heat under the broiler for 3–4 minutes. Spoon a little hummus into each serving dish and top with 3 empanadas and a blood sausage slice. Add a little piquillo pepper coulis and drizzle the parsley oil around. Garnish with a guindilla pepper, pea shoots, and a few Tarbais beans.

FOIE GRAS ROYALE

Royale de foie gras

Serves 4

Active time
1½ hours

Cooking time
1¾ hours

Chilling time
1 hour

Storage
3 days in the refrigerator

Equipment
- Silicone baking mat
- Fine-mesh sieve
- Professional-quality muslin strainer
- Silicone quenelle mold with 1½ × 2½-in. (3.6 × 6.7-cm) cavities
- Steam oven
- Blender
- Piston funnel

Ingredients

Flaxseed nougatine
- 1 cup (6¼ oz./180 g) almonds
- 2½ tbsp (40 ml) water
- 1¼ cups (8½ oz./240 g) superfine sugar
- ½ cup (6¼ oz./180 g) glucose syrup
- Scant ¾ cup (3½ oz./100 g) golden flaxseed

Chicken gelée
- 3½ oz. (100 g) shallots
- ⅓ oz. (10 g) black garlic
- 1 onion
- 2¾ oz. (80 g) carrot
- 4½ lb. (2 kg) chicken wings
- 3½ tbsp (50 ml) peanut oil
- 1 sprig thyme
- 1 bay leaf
- 10 Sarawak black peppercorns
- ¼ cup (2 oz./60 g) egg white (about 2 whites)
- Scant 3 tbsp (1½ oz./40 g) tomato paste
- A few ice cubes
- 12 sheets gelatin (200 Bloom)

Foie gras royale
- 10½ oz. (300 g) raw foie gras
- 1 cup (250 ml) lukewarm whole milk
- 2 eggs
- 3 egg yolks
- Salt and freshly ground pepper

To serve
- Scant ½ cup (100 ml) reduced consommé (from the gelée)
- 3 tsp (10 g) golden flaxseed
- Edible flower petals

PREPARING THE FLAXSEED NOUGATINE

Preheat the oven to 300°F (150°C/Gas Mark 2) and line a baking sheet with the silicone mat. Finely chop the almonds. Heat the water and sugar in a saucepan until the sugar dissolves. Bring to a boil, then stir in the glucose syrup and cook until deeply golden. Stir in the almonds and flaxseed, then spread out on the silicone mat. Cover with parchment paper and roll to a thickness of about ⅛ in. (3 mm). Bake for 5 minutes. Immediately cut out four 6 × 6 × 2-in. (15 × 15 × 5-cm) isosceles triangles. Drape over a rolling pin to give them a curved shape.

PREPARING THE CHICKEN GELÉE

Peel and finely chop the shallots, black garlic, and onion. Peel and slice the carrot. Roughly chop the chicken wings and brown them in a sauté pan with the peanut oil. Drain off excess fat and add the shallots, carrot, thyme, bay leaf, and peppercorns. Add water to just cover and gently simmer for 1 hour. Strain through the fine-mesh sieve into a large heavy-based saucepan. To clarify the stock, whisk the egg whites until frothy, then whisk in the tomato paste, black garlic, and onion. Add a few ice cubes to regulate the temperature. Whisk this mixture into the stock and warm for 10 minutes over medium heat. The egg whites will form a "raft" of solids on the surface, clarifying the broth. Pierce a hole in the center of the "raft" and continue to cook for 30 minutes. Meanwhile, soak the gelatin in a bowl of cold water until softened. Pass the consommé through the muslin strainer and transfer 1¼ cups (300 ml) to a saucepan. Reduce to a syrup-like consistency for serving. Squeeze the gelatin to remove excess water and stir it into the remaining consommé until dissolved. Pour into the quenelle mold and let set for 1 hour in the refrigerator.

PREPARING THE FOIE GRAS ROYALE

Preheat the steam oven to 175°F (80°C/Gas on lowest setting). Devein the foie gras (see technique p. 48) and process in the blender with the milk until smooth. Strain through the fine-mesh sieve, whisk in the eggs and egg yolks, and season with salt and pepper. Using the piston funnel, dispense the royale into 4 soup plates and bake for 30 minutes, until the texture is flan-like.

TO SERVE

Pour a ring of reduced consommé around the edge of each warm royale and sprinkle with flaxseed. Place a piece of nougatine and a gelée quenelle in the center. Garnish with a flower petal.

CRISPY PIGS' EARS

Oreilles de cochon croustillantes

Serves 6

Active time
1 hour

Cooking time
2½ hours

Storage
5 days in the refrigerator

Equipment
Razor
¾ × 5-in. (2 × 12-cm) mold, ¾ in. (2 cm) deep
Fine-mesh sieve
2 small parchment paper piping cones

Ingredients

Pigs' ears
3 pigs' ears
1 onion
3 whole cloves
1 carrot, halved
1 bouquet garni
Coarse grey sea salt

Reduced stock
Pigs' ear cooking stock (see above)
4 tsp (20 ml) sherry vinegar

To garnish
1 green mango
4 tsp (20 ml) grape-seed oil
⅓ cup (1¾ oz./50 g) unsalted peanuts
2 tsp (10 g) *moutarde violette de Brive* (Brive violet mustard)

To serve
A few celery leaves

PREPARING THE PIGS' EARS

Using the razor, shave the hairs off the pigs' ears and rinse well. To blanch the ears, place them in a large saucepan of cold salted water and bring to a boil. Let simmer for 20 minutes, skimming off any foam that rises to the surface. Peel the onion, stick the cloves into it, and add to the pan with the carrot, bouquet garni, and salt. Cook at a gentle simmer for 2 hours, until the ears are tender. Remove them from the pot, reserving the stock. Remove the thick cartilage at the base of the ears and cut the rest into thin slices about ½ in. (1 cm) wide. Line the mold with plastic wrap and arrange the ear slices inside. Press down firmly.

PREPARING THE REDUCED STOCK

Strain the stock through the fine-mesh sieve into a saucepan and reduce until thick and syrupy. Deglaze with the sherry vinegar, then transfer to a parchment paper cone.

PREPARING THE GARNISHES

Peel the green mango, cut the flesh into julienne and gently toss with the grape-seed oil. Toast the peanuts in an ungreased skillet over medium heat for 5 minutes. Stir the mustard to loosen it and spoon into the second parchment paper cone.

TO SERVE

Turn the pigs' ears out of the mold and cut into ¾-in. (2-cm) slices. Caramelize on both sides in an ungreased nonstick skillet. Arrange the slices on serving plates and pipe alternating dots of stock and *moutarde violette* around them. Top with green mango, peanuts, and a few celery leaves.

BEEF CHEEK CROMESQUIS WITH PARSLEY FOAM

Cromesquis de joue de bœuf et espuma au persil

Serves 10

Active time

3 hours

Cooking time

2 hours

Chilling time

1 hour

Standing time (for parsley foam)

30 minutes

Storage

2 days in the refrigerator, after coating with bread crumbs

Equipment

Boning knife

Fine-mesh sieve

10 × 2-in. (5-cm) ring molds, 1¼ in. (3 cm) deep

Food processor

Instant-read thermometer

Immersion blender

Whipping siphon + 2 N_2O gas cartridges

Deep fryer

Ingredients

Beef cheeks

2 beef cheeks *(joues de boeuf)*

Butter

Canola oil

1 carrot, peeled and cut into ½-in. (1-cm) dice

1 onion, peeled and cut into ½-in. (1-cm) dice

2 stalks celery, cut into ½-in. (1-cm) dice

1 bay leaf

3 sprigs thyme

2 cups (500 ml) full-bodied red wine

About 4 cups (1 liter) water

1 tsp tarragon mustard (or to taste)

2 tbsp finely chopped parsley

Salt and freshly ground pepper

Bread crumb coating

¾ cup plus 2 tbsp (3½ oz./100 g) flour

Scant ½ cup (3½ oz./100 g) egg white (about 3 whites), lightly beaten

3½ cups (3½ oz./100 g) dried bread crumbs

Parsley coulis

½ bunch parsley

Scant ⅓ cup (70 ml) water

Parsley foam

1 stick plus 2 tbsp (5¼ oz./150 g) butter

3 eggs

⅓ cup (3 oz./90 g) egg yolk (about 4½ yolks)

⅔ cup (150 ml) olive oil

2 cloves garlic, finely chopped

2 tbsp parsley coulis (see above)

To serve

Oil for deep-frying

A few handfuls mesclun greens

Generous ¾ cup (200 ml) reduced pan juices

⅔ oz. (20 g) fresh black truffle, cut into julienne strips

PREPARING THE BEEF CHEEKS

Preheat the oven to 350°F (180°C/Gas Mark 4). Using the boning knife, trim off the tough sinew and fat from the tops of the beef cheeks. Season with salt and pepper. In a Dutch oven, brown the meat in a little butter and canola oil over medium-high heat. Reduce the heat to low and add the carrot, onion, celery, bay leaf, and thyme. Cook until the vegetables are softened. Deglaze the pan with the red wine, then add enough water to cover the meat halfway. Bring to a boil, skim off any foam, then cover and place in the oven for 1½ hours, or until the beef cheeks are fall-apart tender. Drain the meat, reserving the pan juices, place the meat in a bowl and shred using a fork. Strain the pan juices through the fine-mesh sieve into a saucepan and reduce until syrupy. Stir a scant ½ cup (100 ml) of the reduced juices into the shredded meat to bind it, and reserve the rest for serving. Stir in the mustard and parsley.

PREPARING THE BREAD CRUMB COATING

Place the ring molds on a baking sheet lined with parchment paper and fill with the beef cheek mixture. Let set in the refrigerator for 1 hour. Remove the rings from the meat and coat with flour, shaking off any excess. Dip into the egg white, then coat thoroughly with bread crumbs. Chill until ready to fry.

PREPARING THE PARSLEY COULIS

Cook the parsley briefly in a large saucepan of boiling salted water, then drain. Puree with the scant ⅓ cup (70 ml) water in the food processor.

PREPARING THE PARSLEY FOAM

Melt the butter and let cool to 86°F (30°C). Combine the eggs and egg yolks in a large bowl, then add the butter, olive oil, and garlic. Using the immersion blender, process until smooth. Add the parsley coulis, process again, then strain through the fine-mesh sieve. Transfer to the siphon, charge with the two cartridges, and place in a hot water bath maintained at 136°F (58°C) for about 30 minutes. Shake the siphon before using.

TO SERVE

Preheat the oven to 400°F (200°C/Gas Mark 6). Heat the oil for deep-frying to 340°F (170°C), add the cromesquis, and fry until golden. Finish cooking in the oven for 4 minutes. Dispense a little parsley foam onto each serving plate. Place the cromesquis in the center of the foam and top with mesclun greens. Just before serving, drizzle the reheated reserved pan juices around the cromesquis and top the greens with a little truffle julienne.

SCOTCH EGGS AND MINTED MASHED PEAS

Scotch eggs et écrasé de petits pois à la menthe

Serves 6

Active time
45 minutes

Cooking time
About 1 hour

Chilling time
30 minutes

Storage
2 days in the refrigerator, after coating with bread crumbs

Equipment
Food processor
Food processor with a heating element (Thermomix, see Chefs' Notes)
Fine-mesh sieve
Meat grinder + large plate
Deep fryer
Instant-read thermometer

Ingredients

Minted mashed peas
1 lb. (500 g) fresh peas in their pods
5 tbsp (3 oz./80 g) lightly salted butter
2 tbsp (30 ml) olive oil
15 leaves fresh mint
Juice of ½ lemon
1 tsp (4 g) salt

Pea oil
5 oz. (150 g) empty pea pods (leftover from the mashed peas)
Scant ½ cup (100 ml) olive oil
Scant ½ cup (100 ml) grape-seed oil
1 tsp (4 g) kosher salt

Hard-boiled eggs
4 cups (1 liter) water
Scant ½ cup (100 ml) white vinegar
6 large organic eggs

Farce
1¼ lb. (600 g) pork belly (*poitrine de porc*)
3 anchovy fillets
1 tbsp (3 g) dried oregano
1 tsp (2 g) *pimentón de la Vera* (smoked paprika)
1¾ tsp (9 g) salt

Bread crumb coating
¾ cup plus 2 tbsp (3½ oz./100 g) flour
Scant ½ cup (3½ oz./100 g) egg white (about 3 whites), lightly beaten
3½ cups (3½ oz./100 g) dried bread crumbs

For cooking
Oil for deep-frying

To serve
Extra cooked peas
Pea shoots

CHEFS' NOTES

If you do not have a food processor with a heating element, make the pea oil in the oven, preheated to 160°F (70°C/Gas on lowest setting). Place the pods, oils, and salt in an oven-safe pan, cover, and cook for 40 minutes. Blend until smooth, then strain and chill.

PREPARING THE MINTED MASHED PEAS

Shell the peas, reserving the pods for the pea oil. Cook the peas in a pan of boiling salted water for 5 minutes, then drain. Place them in the food processor with the butter, olive oil, mint, lemon juice, and salt and process to a coarse puree. Taste and adjust the seasonings if necessary. Set aside.

PREPARING THE PEA OIL

Cut the pea pods into small pieces and place in the food processor with a heating element. Add the oils and salt and cook for 40 minutes at 160°F (70°C) on speed 2. Strain through the fine-mesh sieve and chill.

PREPARING THE HARD-BOILED EGGS

In a saucepan, bring the water and vinegar to a boil. Add the eggs and simmer for 5 minutes. Drain, plunge the eggs into a bowl of ice water to stop the cooking, then peel, taking care not to break them.

PREPARING THE FARCE

Cut the pork belly into pieces and grind through the meat grinder with the anchovies into a bowl. Stir in the oregano, *pimentón*, and salt, without overmixing.

SHAPING THE SCOTCH EGGS

For each hard-boiled egg, place 3½ oz. (100 g) of the farce in the palm of your hand and flatten it until it is large enough to enclose the egg. Place the egg in the center, then carefully shape the farce around it until the farce is sealed and the egg is perfectly round.

PREPARING THE BREAD CRUMB COATING

Roll each Scotch egg in the flour, then dip into the egg white, letting any excess drip off. Roll in the bread crumbs until thoroughly coated. Chill for 30 minutes.

COOKING THE SCOTCH EGGS

Preheat the oven to 340°F (170°C/Gas Mark 3). Heat oil for deep-frying to 340°F (170°C). Lower the Scotch eggs into the oil and fry until golden. Using a skimmer, remove the eggs from the oil, put them on a baking sheet, and finish cooking in the oven for 5 minutes.

TO SERVE

Serve the Scotch eggs on a bed of the mashed peas. Accompany with extra cooked peas and garnish with a few pea shoots. Drizzle with the pea oil.

COLD STUFFED RACK OF PORK

Carré de porc froid

Serves 6

Active time

1¾ hours

Cooking time

1½ hours

Resting time

1 month for the cornichons + 3 weeks for the mustard

Storage

5 days in the refrigerator

Equipment

1-qt. (1-liter) jar for the cornichons

1-qt. (1-liter) jar for the mustard

Steam oven

Large sous vide bag + vacuum sealer machine

Sous vide thermometer and probe

Ingredients

Grandmother's cornichons

2¼ lb. (1 kg) fresh cornichon cucumbers

3½ oz. (100 g) additive-free kosher salt

10 peppercorns

10 coriander seeds

½ bunch tarragon

1 sprig thyme

1 bay leaf

1 bird's eye chili pepper

4 juniper berries

3 tsp (10 g) mustard seeds

4 cups (1 liter) white vinegar

Wholegrain mustard

⅔ cup (3½ oz./100 g) brown mustard seeds

⅔ cup (3½ oz./100 g) yellow mustard seeds

1½ tsp (10 g) honey

2 tsp (5 g) ground turmeric

Scant 1 tsp (2 g) xanthan gum

Generous ¾ cup (200 ml) apple cider vinegar, lukewarm

Salt

Chorizo-stuffed rack of pork

9 oz. (250 g) Spanish chorizo

6½ lb. (3 kg) rack of pork (*carré de cochon*), chine bone removed and Frenched

Salt and freshly ground pepper

To serve

Yellow mustard

Toast

PREPARING GRANDMOTHER'S CORNICHONS (1 MONTH AHEAD)

Wash the cucumbers, rub them with the kosher salt, and let sit for 30 minutes to draw out excess moisture. Rinse well with water, dry with a clean dish towel, and place in the cornichon jar with the remaining ingredients minus the vinegar. Heat the vinegar to lukewarm, pour into the jar, close the jar, and turn it upside down until cold to create an airtight seal. Store for 1 month before consuming.

PREPARING THE WHOLEGRAIN MUSTARD (3 WEEKS AHEAD)

To blanch the brown and yellow mustard seeds, place in a saucepan of cold water, bring to a boil, and drain. Repeat twice more. In a large saucepan, warm the honey, turmeric, and xanthan gum. Add the mustard seeds and vinegar and season with salt to taste. Transfer to the jar and place in the refrigerator for 3 weeks before using.

PREPARING THE CHORIZO-STUFFED PORK

Remove the casing from the chorizo and freeze until just frozen. Preheat the steam oven to 185°F (85°C/Gas on lowest setting). Using a knife, bore a hole with the same diameter as the chorizo through the center of the pork fillet and insert the chorizo into the hole. Season the rack with salt and pepper, place in the sous vide bag, and vacuum seal. Cook in the steam oven for 1½ hours or until the center reaches 162°F (72°C). Let cool in the bag over a bed of ice.

TO SERVE

Serve the cold pork sliced, with the cornichons, wholegrain mustard, yellow mustard, and toast on the side.

9.47

MARINATED PORK BELLY WITH PIPERADE, CHORIZO, AND MIRRORED EGG

Lard paysan, piperade, chorizo et œuf miroir

Serves 10

Active time

1 hour

Cooking time

About 4 hours

Resting time

1 hour

Chilling time

2 hours

Storage

5 days in the refrigerator, after cooking

Equipment

Food processor

Instant-read thermometer

2-in. (5-cm) round cookie cutter

Ingredients

Marinade

Generous 3/4 cup (200 ml) maple syrup

Generous 3/4 cup (200 ml) sweet soy sauce

Scant 1/2 cup (100 ml) apple juice

Scant 1/2 cup (100 ml) apple cider vinegar

1 3/4 oz. (50 g) fresh ginger, peeled and chopped

2 cloves garlic, peeled

Pork belly

6 1/2 lb. (3 kg) pork belly (*poitrine de porc*)

Olive oil

Marinade (see above)

Salt

Piperade

4 red bell peppers

4 green bell peppers

1 red onion

Olive oil

2 1/2 oz. (70 g) cured Spanish chorizo, cut into julienne strips

2 tbsp pitted Taggiasca olives, halved

2 tbsp chopped parsley

Piment d'Espelette

Salt

Bell pepper condiment

1 red bell pepper

1/2 red onion, unpeeled

2 cloves garlic

2/3 oz. (20 g) sandwich bread

Oil for deep-frying

2 generous tbsp (20 g) blanched whole almonds

2 generous tbsp (20 g) skinned whole hazelnuts

Piment d'Espelette or smoked paprika

1 tbsp (15 ml) sherry vinegar

Olive oil

Garnishes

3 uncured Spanish chorizo

Olive oil

10 eggs

To serve

Pea shoots

Herb-infused oil (optional)

Piment d'Espelette

PREPARING THE MARINADE

Combine the maple syrup, soy sauce, apple juice, vinegar, ginger, and garlic in the food processor and process until smooth.

PREPARING THE PORK BELLY

Preheat the oven to 285°F (140°C/Gas Mark 1). Remove the skin from the pork belly. Brown the meat all over in an oven-safe skillet with a little olive oil over high heat. Season with salt. Pour over the marinade, cover the skillet with a lid, and place in the oven for about 2½ hours, depending on the thickness of the pork, until the temperature at the center of the meat reaches 160°F (71°C). Let the meat rest at room temperature for 1 hour, then place a weight on top and chill for 2 hours. Using a spoon, scoop the excess fat off the surface of the pan juices. Reduce the remaining juices to a syrup-like consistency.

PREPARING THE PIPERADE

Peel and finely chop the bell peppers and red onion, then sauté in a skillet with a little olive oil over medium heat until softened and browned. Stir in the chorizo, olives, parsley, and *piment d'Espelette*. Season with salt and remove from the heat.

PREPARING THE BELL PEPPER CONDIMENT

Preheat the oven to 350°F (180°C/Gas Mark 4). Wrap the bell pepper, onion, and garlic in parchment paper and roast for 1 hour until cooked. Peel all three, remove the stalk and seeds from the pepper, and place in the food processor. Cut the sandwich bread into ¾-in. (2-cm) cubes and deep-fry with the almonds and hazelnuts until golden. Drain on paper towel. Place in the food processor and add the *piment d'Espelette* or smoked paprika and sherry vinegar. Process until smooth. With the motor running, gradually drizzle in enough olive oil to obtain a thick puree. Let cool, correct the seasonings, and chill until serving.

PREPARING THE GARNISHES

Immediately before serving, preheat the oven to 325°F (160°C/Gas Mark 3). Quickly sear the chorizo all over in a nonstick oven-safe skillet with a little olive oil. Place in the oven for 10 minutes to finish cooking. Cut into 10 slices. Cut the pork belly lengthwise into ¾-in. (2-cm) slices. Trim off the ends at an angle, then sear the slices on both sides in a skillet over high heat. Place in the oven for a few minutes with a little of the pan juices to warm through. In a separate skillet, fry the eggs with a little olive oil for 3–4 minutes, sunny side up, over medium heat. Remove and place on a plate. Using the cookie cutter, cut around the yolks to obtain clean edges.

TO SERVE

Place a slice of pork belly in the center of each serving plate and top with a fried egg. Place a quenelle of piperade and a chorizo slice on one side and a little bell pepper condiment on the other side. Garnish with a few pea shoots, then drizzle a little herb-infused oil around the plate, if using, and dust with *piment d'Espelette*.

BRAISED HAM

Jambon braisé

Serves 4

Active time
10 minutes

Cooking time
3 hours 20 minutes

Storage
4 days in the refrigerator

Equipment
Thin-bladed knife

Ingredients

Braised ham

- 6½-lb. (3-kg) ham, preferably milk-fed
- Coarse grey sea salt, as needed
- Freshly ground pepper
- Olive oil

Glaze

- Scant ½ cup (5 oz./150 g) acacia honey
- 3 tbsp (1¾ oz./50 g) butter
- 2 tsp (10 ml) soy sauce

PREPARING THE BRAISED HAM

Preheat the oven to 400°F (200°C/Gas Mark 6). Using the thin-bladed knife, score the ham skin in a criss-cross pattern, then pierce all over. Rub the outside with coarse grey sea salt, pressing it into the scored pattern. Season with pepper and place in a baking dish. Drizzle with a little olive oil and bake for 40 minutes, then cover with aluminum foil and continue to bake for 1 hour. Lower the oven temperature to 290°F (145°C/Gas Mark 1) and bake for an additional 1 hour.

GLAZING THE HAM

Warm the honey, butter, and soy sauce in a saucepan until liquefied. Remove the ham from the oven and increase the oven temperature to 350°F (180°C/Gas Mark 4). When the oven reaches this temperature, brush the glaze over the ham and bake for 12 minutes. Repeat this process twice more until the ham is glossy and golden brown, and the meat comes away easily from the bone.

PORK TONGUE WITH NORI, CILANTRO CREAM SAUCE, AND OYSTERS

Langues de porc, feuilles de nori, crème de coriandre et huîtres

Serves 4

Active time
1 hour

Cooking time
2 hours

Chilling time
1 hour

Storage
3 days in the refrigerator (before assembling)

Equipment
Fine-mesh sieve
Blender

Ingredients

Pork tongue rolls

- 5 pork tongues (*langues de porc*)
- 1 onion
- 3 whole cloves
- 1 carrot, halved
- 1 bouquet garni
- Scant ½ cup (100 ml) white vinegar
- Coarse grey sea salt
- 4 sheets gelatin (200 Bloom)
- 6 sheets nori

Cilantro cream sauce

- 1 bunch cilantro
- 1¾ oz. (50 g) shallots
- 1¾ oz. (50 g) celery
- 2 tbsp (30 ml) olive oil, divided
- 4 tsp (20 ml) Noilly Prat vermouth
- 4 tsp (20 ml) heavy cream, min. 35% fat

To serve

- 4 oysters, preferably Cadoret No. 3
- Marigold petals

PREPARING THE PORK TONGUE ROLLS

To blanch the tongues, place them in a large saucepan of cold salted water and bring to a boil. Let simmer for 20 minutes, skimming off any foam that rises to the surface. Peel the onion, stick the cloves into it, and add to the pan with the carrot, bouquet garni, vinegar, and coarse grey sea salt. Simmer gently for 1 hour, until the tongues are tender and show little to no resistance when pierced with a knife. Remove the tongues, then strain the broth through the fine-mesh sieve into a saucepan and reduce by two-thirds. Meanwhile, soak the gelatin in a bowl of cold water until softened. Cut the tongues lengthwise into 1¼ × 4-in. (3 × 10-cm) strips. Squeeze the gelatin to remove excess water and stir it into the hot reduced stock until dissolved. Brush a little water over the nori sheets to moisten and line up 2 strips of tongue end to end down the center of each sheet. Roll the nori up tightly, then trim off the ends. Place the rolls close together and cover with plastic wrap to make a single tight cylinder. Chill for 1 hour.

PREPARING THE CILANTRO CREAM SAUCE

Wash the cilantro and remove the leaves, reserving the stems. Cook the leaves in a large saucepan of boiling salted water for 5 minutes, then drain and let cool. Finely chop the cilantro stems, peel and finely chop the shallot, and thinly slice the celery. Add all three to a skillet with 2 tsp (10 ml) of the olive oil and cook over medium-low heat until softened. Deglaze with the vermouth and reduce slightly, then stir in the cream and bring to a boil. Pour into the blender, add the cilantro leaves, and process until smooth. Add the remaining olive oil, strain through the fine-mesh sieve into a bowl, and set the bowl over ice.

TO SERVE

Shuck the oysters. Remove the plastic wrap from the pork tongue roll and cut crosswise into 2-in. (5-cm) slices. Place a slice in the center of each serving bowl and pour cilantro cream sauce around it. Top with an oyster and garnish with a few marigold petals.

PIKE QUENELLES WITH SPICY BISQUE

Quenelles de brochet et bisque épicée

Serves 6

Active time
40 minutes

Cooking time
1 hour 50 minutes

Chilling time
30 minutes

Freezing time
20 minutes

Storage
3 days in the refrigerator (see Chefs' Notes)

Equipment
Food processor
Fine-mesh sieve
Instant-read thermometer
2 quenelle spoons

Ingredients

Pike quenelles
Scant 1/2 cup (100 ml) mussel juices (or use white chicken stock)
2 tbsp (1 oz./30 g) butter
1 3/4 tsp (9 g) salt, divided
3/4 tsp (2 g) ground black pepper, divided
2/3 cup (3 oz./80 g) all-purpose flour
9 oz. (250 g) skinned pike fillet
3 eggs
5 tbsp (3 oz./80 g) butter, softened

Spicy bisque
3 oz. (75 g) fennel
3 1/2 oz. (100 g) shallots
13 oz. (375 g) tomatoes
1 1/2 lb. (750 g) rock fish carcasses
3 1/2 tbsp (50 ml) olive oil
2 tbsp (25 g) butter
2 1/2 tbsp (1 1/2 oz./40 g) tomato paste
1/4 cup (60 ml) cognac
1/2 cup (125 ml) white wine
1 1/2 cups (375 ml) white chicken stock (*fond blanc de volaille*)
2/3 cup (150 ml) heavy cream
Scant 1/2 tsp (1 g) Cayenne pepper

To serve
Grated Parmesan
A few small salad leaves, such as purple oxalis
Olive oil

PREPARING THE PIKE QUENELLES

In a saucepan over low heat, warm the mussel juices with the 2 tablespoons (1 oz./30 g) butter, a generous 1/2 teaspoon (3 g) of the salt, and half the pepper. When the mixture comes to a boil, add the flour and cook for 3 minutes over low heat, stirring constantly with a spatula. Transfer to a dish, press plastic wrap over the surface, and chill until cold and firm. Cut the pike fillet into 3/4-in. (2-cm) dice and freeze for 20 minutes, until firm. Separate the pieces, if necessary, place in the food processor with the mussel juice and flour mixture, and add the remaining salt and pepper. Process for about 20 seconds to release the fish proteins and ensure a smooth texture. Incorporate the eggs one at a time, then mix in the softened butter. Transfer to a bowl, press plastic wrap over the surface, and chill until cooking.

PREPARING THE SPICY BISQUE

Wash and thinly slice the fennel and peel and thinly slice the shallots. Wash and quarter the tomatoes. Roughly chop the fish carcasses and brown in a skillet with the olive oil and butter over medium-high heat. Add the fennel and shallots and cook until lightly golden, then stir in the tomato paste. Deglaze with the cognac and white wine and reduce slightly. Add the tomatoes and chicken stock and cook over low heat for 1 hour, then stir in the cream and Cayenne pepper and cook for an additional 30 minutes. Strain through the fine-mesh sieve into a clean saucepan and, if necessary, reduce until the bisque coats the back of a spoon.

COOKING THE QUENELLES

Pour 4 cups (1 liter) water into a large saucepan and season generously with salt. Heat to 195°F (90°C) and keep the temperature steady as you cook the quenelles. Stir the quenelle mixture using a spatula to loosen it. Using the quenelle spoons, shape the mixture into 6 quenelles and drop them into the hot water. Cook for 15 minutes, turning them regularly.

TO SERVE

Using a skimmer, transfer the quenelles to a baking sheet lined with parchment paper. Sprinkle with Parmesan and place briefly under the broiler, until lightly golden. Fill the bases of 6 soup plates with bisque and place a quenelle in the center of each plate. Decorate with small salad leaves of your choice and finish with a few drops of olive oil.

CHEFS' NOTES

If you wish to freeze the quenelles, cook them as indicated, then plunge into ice-cold water to cool them down quickly. Drain and open freeze on a baking sheet lined with plastic wrap, then transfer to an airtight freezer bag and store for up to 1 month.

PORK CHEEK TERRINE WITH LEEKS AND RAVIGOTE SAUCE

Joues de cochon, poireaux et ravigote

Serves 4

Active time
2 hours

Cooking time
1 hour

Chilling time
2 hours

Storage
3 days in the refrigerator

Equipment
Fine-mesh sieve
Triangular terrine mold, 2¾ in. (7 cm) deep

Ingredients

Pork cheeks
- 1 carrot
- 1 onion
- 1 lb. 2 oz. (500 g) pork cheeks (*joues de cochon*)
- 1 sprig thyme
- 1 bay leaf
- 5 black peppercorns
- 3 whole cloves
- 3½ tbsp (50 ml) white wine
- Coarse grey sea salt

Leeks
- 6 thin spring leeks
- Coarse grey sea salt

Ravigote sauce
- 1 egg
- 1¾ oz. (50 g) shallots
- ¼ bunch tarragon
- ¼ bunch chervil
- 3½ tbsp (50 ml) apple cider vinegar
- 2 tsp (10 g) tarragon mustard
- Scant ½ cup (100 ml) grape-seed oil
- Salt and freshly ground pepper

To serve
- Oil for deep-frying
- Pansy petals
- Herb-infused oil (optional, see Layered Vegetable and Omelet Terrine recipe, p. 174)

PREPARING THE PORK CHEEKS

Peel and finely chop the carrot and onion. To peel the pork cheeks, run a very sharp knife under the membrane to release it. Place the cheeks in a large saucepan and add enough cold salted water to just cover them. Bring to a boil, skimming off any foam that rises to the surface. Add the carrot, onion, thyme, bay leaf, peppercorns, cloves, and white wine. Season with coarse grey sea salt and simmer gently until the cheeks are tender (35–40 minutes). Remove the cheeks and strain the cooking liquid through the fine-mesh sieve into a clean saucepan. Reduce to a syrup-like consistency.

PREPARING THE LEEKS

Cut the root ends off the leeks, wash under hot water several times to remove dirt, and reserve for garnish. Trim off a little of the green parts, cut into julienne and set aside for garnish. Slice the leeks lengthwise down the center and rinse well under warm water. Cook in a large saucepan of boiling salted water until tender, then plunge into a bowl of ice water. Remove the outermost leaves and reserve for assembling. Cut the leeks into 4-in. (10-cm) lengths and carefully char over a flame or under a preheated 350°F (180°C/Gas Mark 4) broiler for 10 minutes.

ASSEMBLING THE TERRINE

Cut the pork cheeks into 2-in. (5-cm) pieces. Line the triangular mold with the reserved blanched leek leaves and arrange the pork cheek pieces over them. Pour in enough reduced cooking juices to fill the mold and chill for 2 hours.

PREPARING THE RAVIGOTE SAUCE

Cook the egg in boiling water for 9–10 minutes until hard-boiled. Peel and finely chop the shallots. Wash the tarragon and chervil, remove the leaves, and chop finely. Dissolve a little salt in the vinegar and season with pepper. Stir in the mustard, shallot, and herbs. Immediately before serving, peel and press the hard-boiled egg through the sieve into the sauce and stir to combine. Gradually whisk in the oil until emulsified and thick.

TO SERVE

Deep-fry the leek roots and julienned green parts in the oil for a few minutes, until crisp. Arrange charred leek slices on each serving plate, add two thick slices of pork cheek terrine, and drizzle over the ravigote sauce. Garnish with fried leek roots and julienned green parts, and a few pansy petals. If you wish, drizzle a little herb-infused oil around the plate.

SERRANO HAM CROQUETTES

Croquetas au jambon serrano

Serves 10

Active time
1 hour

Cooking time
15 minutes

Chilling time
2 hours

Freezing time
30 minutes

Storage
3–4 days in the refrigerator, before frying

Equipment
Pastry bag + 1/2-in. (1.3-cm) plain tip
Immersion blender
Mini round cookie cutter
Deep fryer

Ingredients

Croquettes
4 oz. (120 g) Serrano ham
2¾ oz. (80 g) goat milk tomme cheese
½ onion
3 tbsp (1¾ oz./50 g) butter
1 cup plus 2 tbsp (5¼ oz./150 g) all-purpose flour
2 cups (500 ml) whole milk
1 egg yolk
½ tsp (1 g) *piment d'Espelette*
Salt

Bread crumb coating
Scant 1 cup (7 oz./200 g) egg white (about 7 whites), lightly beaten
1⅔ cups (7 oz./200 g) all-purpose flour
7 cups (7 oz./200 g) dried bread crumbs

Toum sauce
2½ oz. (70 g) garlic
¼ cup (60 ml) lemon juice
¼ cup (2 oz./60 g) egg white (2 whites)
1¼ cups (300 ml) canola oil

To serve
4 piquillo peppers, from a jar
Oil for deep-frying
A few slices Serrano ham
Pickled guindilla peppers
Deep-fried parsley sprigs

PREPARING THE CROQUETTES

Cut the Serrano ham into thin julienne strips, measuring 1¼–1½ in. (3–4 cm). Roughly chop the cheese. Peel and finely chop the onion. Melt the butter in a large saucepan over low heat, then add the onion and cook for 5 minutes, until softened but not browned. Add the flour to make a roux, then cook for 2 minutes without browning, whisking constantly. Still whisking, gradually pour in the milk and cook for 2 minutes until thick. Remove from the heat, whisk in the egg yolk, then return to the heat. Quickly bring to a boil, remove from the heat again, and stir in the ham, cheese, and *piment d'Espelette*. Season with salt, transfer to a container, and chill for 2 hours. Transfer to the pastry bag and pipe out 5 logs measuring 14 in. (35 cm) in length onto a baking sheet lined with parchment paper. Freeze for 30 minutes, then cut the logs into 25 croquettes, each measuring 2¾ in. (7 cm) in length.

PREPARING THE BREAD CRUMB COATING

Dip each croquette into the egg white to coat, then roll in the flour, followed by the bread crumbs. Dip once more into the egg white, then coat with a second layer of bread crumbs.

PREPARING THE TOUM SAUCE

Peel and remove the germs from the garlic cloves. Plunge them into a pan of boiling water and remove as soon as the water returns to a boil. Place in a bowl with the lemon juice and egg white. Using the immersion blender, process until smooth. With the blender running, very gradually drizzle in the canola oil until the sauce emulsifies and thickens like a mayonnaise. Chill until serving.

TO SERVE

Cut out tiny rounds of piquillo pepper using the mini cutter. Heat oil for deep-frying to 340°F (170°C) and deep-fry the croquettes in batches of 5 until golden brown. Drain on paper towel. Serve the croquettes warm, topped with the piquillo pepper rounds and garnished with thin slices of Serrano ham, guindilla peppers, and crisp-fried parsley sprigs. Spoon the toum sauce into a small bowl for dipping.

FEBRU
12, 2008
Parker
Restaurant
Good news
culinary ico
restaurant,
Mag's Food
gastronomy
Pizzeria spac
food and well-cr
of Parker
hird newborn daughter.
avant-garde
up a second
port from NY
list molecular
the former Muth
The kitchen will serve "modern casual
for the restaurant. The name Roberta is the
Molecula
nomy:
Explori
ience
of fla
An intern
french tel
author, a
chef Vi
doctora
field he
experime
kitchen, us
into the
the chemistry, physics
to challenge traditional ideas
about cooking and eating. What he discovers will
entertain, instruct and intrigue cooks, gourments and

SADDLE OF RABBIT AND PRUNE TERRINE

Râble de lapin gibelotte, condiment de pruneaux

Serves 6

Active time
2 hours

Cooking time
2 hours

Soaking time
30 minutes

Chilling time
Overnight

Storage
5 days in the refrigerator

Equipment
Steam oven (or steamer)
Flat meat tenderizer
Fine-mesh sieve
Instant-read thermometer
Blender
Disposable pastry bag
6 × 8-in. (15 × 20-cm) terrine mold, 5 in. (12 cm) deep

Ingredients

Rabbit saddle
3 rabbit saddles
2/3 oz. (20 g) sumac
Salt and freshly ground pepper

Gibelotte stock
2 carrots
7 oz. (200 g) shallots
1 bunch tarragon
1 bouquet garni
5 peppercorns
Scant 1/2 cup (100 ml) dry white wine
12 sheets gelatin (200 Bloom)

Prune condiment
14 oz. (400 g) prunes
1 2/3 cups (400 ml) red wine
Generous 3/4 cup (200 ml) spring water
1 cinnamon stick
2 star anise pods
10 sheets gelatin (200 Bloom)
3 1/2 tbsp (50 ml) balsamic vinegar

Vegetables
2 1/4 lb. (1 kg) spinach leaves, plus a few small leaves for garnish
8 mini carrots
Coarse grey sea salt

PREPARING THE RABBIT SADDLE

Preheat the steam oven to 200°F (100°C/Gas Mark 1/4). Debone the rabbit saddles, reserving the bones for the stock. Remove the loins and season with sumac, salt, and pepper. Cover each loin with plastic wrap and shape into cylinders. Cook in the steam oven (or steamer) for 10–15 minutes, then chill for 30 minutes.

PREPARING THE GIBELOTTE STOCK

Crush the saddle bones with the meat tenderizer. Peel and chop the carrots and shallots. Wash and roughly chop the tarragon. Place all three in a Dutch oven with the bones, bouquet garni, peppercorns, and wine. Simmer gently for 1 hour. Meanwhile, soak the gelatin in a bowl of cold water until softened. Strain the rabbit stock through the fine-mesh sieve; avoid pressing down to keep the stock clear. When the stock cools to 104°F (40°C), squeeze the gelatin to remove excess water and stir it in until dissolved. Set aside.

PREPARING THE PRUNE CONDIMENT

Soak the prunes in lukewarm water for 30 minutes, until moist and plump. Drain, then place them in a saucepan with the wine, spring water, and spices and let simmer for 20 minutes. Meanwhile, soak the gelatin in a bowl of cold water until softened. Remove the spices, pour the prunes and liquid into a blender, and puree. Strain through the fine-mesh sieve, then stir in the balsamic vinegar. Squeeze the gelatin to remove excess water and stir it in until dissolved. Transfer to the pastry bag.

PREPARING THE VEGETABLES

Cook the spinach in a large pan of boiling salted water until just wilted. Drain, then plunge into a bowl of ice water to preserve the color. Drain and pat dry. Peel the carrots, maintaining their cylindrical shape. Cook in a large saucepan of boiling salted water until just tender. Drain and refresh in ice water.

ASSEMBLING THE TERRINE

Line the inside of the terrine mold with plastic wrap, then line the base and sides with spinach leaves to cover completely. Remove the plastic wrap from the rabbit loins and arrange alternately with the carrots in the mold, piping the prune condiment between them. Pour in rabbit stock to fill the mold and cover with spinach leaves. Cover with plastic wrap and chill overnight. When ready to serve, turn the terrine out of the mold and cut into slices. Serve garnished with small spinach leaves.

SALMON À LA PARISIENNE

Saumon à la parisienne

Serves 4

Active time
2 hours

Resting time
20 minutes

Cooking time
40 minutes

Cooling time
45 minutes

Chilling time
2 hours

Storage
3 days in the refrigerator

Equipment
Steam oven (or steamer)
Instant-read thermometer
Fine-mesh sieve
Melon baller
Pipette

Ingredients

Salmon
4 × 5¼-oz. (150-g) fresh salmon loins, skinned
3 tbsp (1½ oz./40 g) fleur de sel
3½ tbsp (50 ml) olive oil
Salt and freshly ground pepper

Chaudfroid sauce
5¼ oz. (150 g) shallots
1 tbsp (20 g) butter
⅔ cup (150 ml) Noilly Prat vermouth
2 cups (500 ml) fish fumet
6 sheets gelatin (200 Bloom)
Generous ¾ cup (200 ml) heavy cream, min. 35% fat

Vegetable marbles
2 carrots
2 round turnips
2 zucchini
Coarse grey sea salt

To serve
2 tsp (10 g) English mustard
1¾ oz. (50 g) salmon roe
Verbena flowers

PREPARING THE SALMON
Preheat the steam oven to 175°F (80°C/Gas on lowest setting). Remove the pin bones from the salmon, coat with the fleur de sel, and let sit for 20 minutes to draw out moisture. Pat dry with paper towel and brush each loin on both sides with olive oil. Season with salt and pepper, cover each one with plastic wrap, and cook in the steam oven (or steamer) for 10 minutes, until the temperature in the center reaches 82°F (28°C). Let cool for 45 minutes at room temperature, then remove the plastic wrap, pat dry, and place on a rack.

PREPARING THE CHAUDFROID SAUCE
Peel and finely chop the shallots, then sweat in a large sauté pan with the butter until softened. Deglaze with the vermouth, reduce, and add the fish fumet. Cook for 20 minutes. Meanwhile, soak the gelatin in a bowl of cold water until softened. Stir the cream into the pan and bring to a boil, then strain through the fine-mesh sieve into a bowl. Squeeze the gelatin to remove excess water and stir it into the hot mixture until dissolved. Let cool to 77°F (25°C), then use to glaze the salmon loins. Chill for 2 hours.

PREPARING THE VEGETABLE MARBLES
Wash the vegetables, peel the carrots and turnips, and cut out "marbles" from all three using the melon baller. Cook each vegetable separately in a saucepan of boiling salted water until just tender. Drain, then let cool completely.

TO SERVE
Stir a little water into the English mustard to thin it out, place in the pipette, and pipe out a zigzag pattern across each serving plate. Place a salmon loin in the center and arrange vegetable marbles at either end. Garnish with salmon roe and a few verbena flowers.

APPENDIXES

INDEX

INDEX (continued)

Acknowledgments

We would like to thank
Marine Mora and the **Matfer Bourgeat Group**
as well as the **Mora** store for the utensils and equipment.
www.matferbourgeat.com
www.mora.fr

Rina Nurra extends her warmest thanks to:
Clélia Ozier-Lafontaine and Audrey Janet for their trust and constant support.
Chefs Marc Alès, Stéphane Jakic, and Frédéric Lesourd, with whom it is always a pleasure to work, both on an aesthetic and a gustatory level.
Marie Nurra, for her inspiring ceramic creations, created specially for this book.